ROUTLEDGE LIBRARY EDITIONS: COLONIALISM AND IMPERIALISM

Volume 37

MALTA AND THE END OF EMPIRE

MALTA AND THE END OF EMPIRE

DENNIS AUSTIN

LONDON AND NEW YORK

First published in 1971 by Frank Cass & Company Limited

This edition first published in 2023
by Routledge
4 Park Square, Milton Park, Abingdon, Oxon OX14 4RN

and by Routledge
605 Third Avenue, New York, NY 10158

Routledge is an imprint of the Taylor & Francis Group, an informa business

© 1971 Dennis Austin

All rights reserved. No part of this book may be reprinted or reproduced or utilised in any form or by any electronic, mechanical, or other means, now known or hereafter invented, including photocopying and recording, or in any information storage or retrieval system, without permission in writing from the publishers.

Trademark notice: Product or corporate names may be trademarks or registered trademarks, and are used only for identification and explanation without intent to infringe.

British Library Cataloguing in Publication Data
A catalogue record for this book is available from the British Library

ISBN: 978-1-032-41054-8 (Set)
ISBN: 978-1-032-43402-5 (Volume 37) (hbk)
ISBN: 978-1-032-43414-8 (Volume 37) (pbk)
ISBN: 978-1-003-36718-5 (Volume 37) (ebk)

DOI: 10.4324/9781003367185

Publisher's Note
The publisher has gone to great lengths to ensure the quality of this reprint but points out that some imperfections in the original copies may be apparent.

Disclaimer
The publisher has made every effort to trace copyright holders and would welcome correspondence from those they have been unable to trace.

Malta and the End of Empire

Dennis Austin
*Professor of Government,
University of Manchester*

**FRANK CASS & CO. LTD.
1971**

First published in 1971 by
FRANK CASS & COMPANY LIMITED
67, Great Russell Street, London WC1B 3BT

Copyright © 1971 DENNIS AUSTIN

ISBN 0 7146 2774 7

All Rights Reserved. No part of this publication may be reproduced in any form or by any means, electronic, mechanical, photo-copying, recording or otherwise, without the prior permission of Frank Cass and Company Limited in writing.

Printed in the Republic of Ireland by Cahill & Co. Limited, Parkgate Printing Works, Dublin

"On this important day in the history of the British Commonwealth we meet to consider the affairs of the lovely islands of Malta and Gozo."

Alan Lennox Boyd, H.C. Deb., 26 March, 1956.

Where are the eagles and the trumpets?

Il doutait de tout, même de l'empire.

Contents

Preface	xi
I. L'Angleterre d'Outre-mer?	1
II. The 1956 Referendum	25
III. Separation	63
Notes	112
Select Bibliography	129
Index	131

List of Illustrations

facing page

1. Dom Mintoff in 1955	52
2. Borg Olivier in 1956	52
3. Archbishop Michael Gonzi (photographed in 1964)	53
4. Lord Strickland (1861–1940)	53
5. Mabel Strickland and Paul Boffa	68
6. Mabel Strickland addressing a political meeting	68
7. A contested election, 1955	69
8. Map of the Maltese islands	110–111

Acknowledgements are due to The Associated Press Ltd. for photographs 1, 2, 6, and 7; to United Press International (U.K.) Ltd. for photograph 3; to Bassano and Vandyk Studios for photograph 4; and to the Radio Times Hulton Picture Library for photograph 5.

Preface

ALTHOUGH the events set out in these pages happened not many years ago, they already belong to a remote imperial age which is hardly remembered today. I hope the reader will not be deterred by that, since it is an easy tale, lightly told, with an occasional undertone of serious comment in the third part of the essay where I have examined the British side to Anglo-Maltese relations during the argument about integration in 1955-56.

The inquiry arose by chance out of a visit to the Maltese islands for quite different purposes. My interest in the integration proposals, which the prime minister of Malta, Mr. Dom Mintoff, put forward in 1955, was kindled by two articles in *International Affairs* and *Political Studies* on 'The End of Empire' and 'Alternatives to Independence', both by Professor Kenneth Robinson, then at Nuffield College, Oxford. I read them in the aeroplane during the short flight from London to Valletta. They examined the possibility of an end to empire by the absorption of a colony into the state system of the imperial power: as successive French governments had attempted to do in terms of *la France d'Outre-mer,* and as Portugal, much less plausibly, was still asserting it was trying to bring about in its overseas provinces. The argument was ingenious. But was it really true that the British had moved timidly in the same direction? I had thought

Malta and the End of Empire

that imperial federation was dead and gone, and with O'Leary in the grave. Had it really been resurrected in the 1950s? I began to inquire further, into newspapers, books and pamphlets in the Royal Library, Valletta; talked to party leaders and other notables in Malta and Gozo, returned to Britain, went to Rome, revisited Malta, searched about, and wrote each of the three sections of the essay in the time available to me while moving from London to Manchester in 1968-69.

Now all that remains to be said in this brief preface, before turning to examine what took place between these years, is to thank those who helped to tell the tale and make it worth the telling. It is a pleasant duty indeed to make public my thanks to Miss Mabel Strickland, Chev. Joseph Galea, Victor Gauci, Mr. Dom Mintoff, Mr. Philip Saliba, Edgar and Mary Mangeon, Richard Matrenza, and many other denizens of those happy islands. I should also like to thank a number of friends in Britain—Deborah Lavin, Hermia Oliver, Professor Gerald Graham, Dr. Anirudha Gupta, Dr. Peter Lyon, Professor Morris-Jones, Andrew Shonfield, William Tordoff, and others who listened tolerantly to talk about Malta and offered comments on the text.

The money for these inquiries came very generously from London University and Shell International. And not one of the pages in this short essay would have seen the light of day without the great help uncomplainingly given by my secretary, Joyce Ingham.

D.A.

MANCHESTER
15th March, 1970

PART I

L'Angleterre d'Outre-mer?

TOWARDS the beginning of 1956 a singular event befell the people of the three islands: Malta, Gozo and Comino. They were asked by the Maltese and British Governments to decide whether they wanted "full integration" with the United Kingdom, a remarkable proposal which ran quite contrary to the general movement of colonial policy at the time. In the fifteen years which have elapsed since the offer was made, it has never been repeated, and one may reasonably assume that the proposals agreed to by both governments were no more than a momentary interruption of the now familiar story of emancipation from colonial rule. But it is always interesting, even enjoyable, when the unexpected happens and a course of events which seems set unswervingly in a particular direction is disturbed. Ah, one can say, nothing is inevitable in history. There are always alternatives: even to the end of empire; and alternatives so different from the normal fate of imperial rule as to make one wonder whether it is right to talk about an end at all. It is true that the alternative did not happen. In September 1964 Malta joined the ranks of the newly independent states; but it was very nearly a different story. Elderly imperialists who remembered the debates over Imperial federation which stretched from the end of the last century to the first world war must have rubbed their eyes in wonder when they read that the British government was ready at last to admit a number (a very small number, to be sure) of overseas representatives to the House of Commons, and to extend the frontiers of the United Kingdom in order to include the territory of what was still a "self-governing colony". It was as if a policy well tried out in Paris for *la France d'Outre-mer* had suddenly taken flight and come to rest on the banks of the Thames.

How did it come about? The question can be answered quite simply by re-telling the story of the negotiations. But why? That is more difficult to explain since it raises questions about the nature of British imperialism which can be answered only by conjecture. The second part of this essay examines the easier of the two questions—what actually happened in 1956? The third section is concerned with the United Kingdom and its imperial role. But first we must say something about Malta itself.

The islands are very small. Malta proper is no more than eight by seventeen-and-a-half miles; Gozo four-and-a-half by nine, Comino only a mile square; one can add to these the rocky islets of Cominotto and Filfla which though very beautiful in the haze of a Mediterranean sun are uninhabited and uninhabitable.[1] On this tiny archipelago live over 300,000 people whose numbers are kept within tolerable bounds by large-scale emigration. At the last census in 1967 the total count was 314,175 divided between Comino and Gozo—25,975; and Malta—288,200. The thickest cluster of

L'Angleterre d'Outre-mer?

population—over 3,000 to the square mile—lives in the Inner Harbour Region, from Sliema eastwards to Valletta and the Three Cities of Senglea, Vittoriosa and Cospicua.[2] Towns and villages stand close together, and no part of the main island is more than a short omnibus ride from the capital. Nor is the small island, Gozo, very far from Malta: there is a regular ferry across the three-mile-wide channel, and a fast hydrofoil service between Valletta and the little harbour town of Mgarr.

The Maltese have lived in these islands for a time almost beyond memory. Their history extends certainly to Roman times, and very likely to Carthage and the Phoenicians, Malta having been a sister colony of Carthage within the Punic empires.[3] But if the Phoenicians were among the direct ancestors of the Maltese, the islands themselves were known to much earlier seafarers, builders of the megalithic temples and ossuaries which still stand, marvellously preserved, on Malta and Gozo. The hypogeum of Halsaflieni, and the rock-hewn temples at Tarxien, Hagar Qim, Mnajdra and Ggantija, are magnificent memorials to the first of all the Mediterranean peoples. And one can understand why the islands were so attractive, then as now. They have many advantages: equi-distant from Gibraltar at the western end of the Mediterranean and Alexandria in the east, less than 60 miles from Sicily, less than 200 miles from Africa, a stony but fertile soil,[4] local springs of fresh water, a warm sun, good building stone, easily fortified heights, sheltered bays where ships can ride out a storm, and a safe anchorage both in the harbour at Marsamuscetto and the Grand

Harbour itself—spreading out from its narrow entrance between the two great star forts of St. Elmo and St. Angelo into the long stretch of water below the present city of Valletta. A prize worth taking. And the greater part of Maltese history has been one of wars, blockades, conquest, resistance, victory and defeat under more than 2,000 years of foreign rule. When the Roman Empire divided, Malta fell to Byzantium; when the eastern empire collapsed, Arab control replaced that of the Greeks.[5] The Normans under Roger, Count of Sicily, captured the islands in 1090 and Malta came under the control of the Sicilian Kingdoms—Norman, Angevin, Castile and Aragon. Then in 1530 the Emperor Charles V gave the islands and the Castle of Tripoli to the Order of the Hospital of St. John of Jerusalem, homeless since its eviction from Rhodes by the Turks in 1523. And for almost 250 years the knights of St. John had their headquarters in Valletta after the Great Siege of 1565 when they and the ordinary people of Malta drove back the Turkish invasion force under Dragut.

It was a long, peaceful and, by the standards of the age, beneficent regime which came to an abrupt end when the last Grand Master—the German, Ferdinand Hompesch—capitulated to the French under Napoleon in 1798, until they too were defeated by a mixed force of Maltese and British troops under Captain Ball, R.N. Thus in 1802 Malta came under British rule, and was made a Crown Colony after the Treaty of Paris in 1814, but not a conquered territory, the islands having been ceded freely to the Crown.[6]

Who ruled in Malta? The answer is simple: every-

L'Angleterre d'Outre-mer?

one except on rare occasions of crisis and interregnum the Maltese themselves. The Norman, Spanish and Italian overlords established themselves as a local nobility whose homes and courtyards are there still in the lovely town of Mdina, but they retained their foreign titles and held aloof from the ordinary people. The Knights of St. John kept away from Mdina and ruled the islands from their city on Mt. Sceberras above the Grand Harbour or from Verdala Palace among the cyprus and orange groves at Boschetto. The wealth of the Order, drawn from its estates in Catholic Europe, greatly enriched Valletta and must have benefited indirectly the Maltese themselves. Certainly, the Knights prospered, "prepared" as Gibbon observed, "to die but not to live in the service of Christ". Yet they deserve to be remembered not only for the southern Baroque splendour of their *auberges*[7] and churches but their good works, including the great Aquaduct built by the Grand Master Alof de Wignacourt, and the Sacred Infirmary—an immense hospital ward, over 500 feet in length, 35 feet wide, in which for more than 300 years the standard of medicine was considerably in advance of the greater part of Europe at the time. The Maltese lived on under both sets of rulers, preserved their language, and neither fully accepted nor were wholly hostile to the power of the Knights and the old nobility. What else could they do? It was not yet the age of popular sovereignty and nationalist demands. And even if such notions had been entertained there was the danger of external enemies. The islands were too valuable a strategic prize to be ignored. The Maltese knew it, and learned to adjust their loyalties and fate to whoever offered—or forced upon them—protection.

The reader might well ask what bearing this long sweep of history has on the particular debate over integration in the 1950's. It had a great deal. Indeed, we must now take note of two additional problems born of the long history of these small islands. One was the effect of the early conversion of the Maltese to Christianity, traditionally attributed to St. Paul when shipwrecked on the north-west coast at what is today St. Paul's Bay: a conversion which was total and complete, for the Maltese clung to their Roman Christian beliefs under both Arab and Byzantine rule, and were reinforced in their attachment to Rome by the long residence among them of the Knights of St. John. Over the centuries, the Catholic Church came to control the social and political life of the people until by the end of the nineteenth century Malta was a special object of Papal concern. There was little to hinder the rule of the Church. Even under the British there was no unit of popularly-based, local government, and the priest ruled unchallenged in his local parish. The splendour of St. Paul's cathedral in Mdina, and of the pro-cathedral of St. John in Valletta, was matched by the power of the church hierarchy under its Archbishop, Bishops, and more than a thousand diocesan priests, friars and monks. Malta is a Catholic island and its political life today, as in the past, is dominated by the fact.

The other related element in the recent history of the islands has been the influence of the neighbouring mainland. It was not difficult, certainly many Italians

L'Angleterre d'Outre-mer?

did not find it so, to argue that the Maltese archipelago was an extension of the Italian peninsula—Italy, Sicily, Pantelleria, Gozo, Malta, Lampedusa—and that it was only the historical accident of British naval power in the Mediterranean in the nineteenth century which prevented the possibility of Malta's being drawn into the movement for Italian unification. It is true of course that the British were instrumental in helping to bring the *Risorgimento* to its successful conclusion.[8] But gratitude in history is short-lived. Nor was it perhaps unreasonable to assume that if the power of Britain were to decline, or be broken, that of Italy might take its place as the dominant influence in the central Mediterranean. The argument was later to be advanced with a shrill vehemence under Mussolini, but already by the end of the last century the "Italianate element" in Malta was strong, and seemed likely to grow. Many of the leaders of the small bourgeois class in Valletta and Mdina looked to Italy as their cultural homeland; they preferred to speak Italian rather than English or Maltese in public affairs. And the language of the church, law courts, university,[9] the National Assembly, the schools, and some of the local newspapers, was Italian.

The leader of the "Italian faction" for nearly half a century was Dr. Enrico Mizzi, a remarkable man whose career was not unlike that of the fortunes of Malta itself. His father Fortunato Mizzi was Maltese, his mother Italian: both father and son were lawyers by profession, and able politicians, whose passionate advocacy of the need for closer ties with Italy, their love of Italian culture, and Enrico Mizzi's admiration in the 1920s and '30s for Mussolini, brought them into conflict with the colonial government as guardian of the "fortress colony". The elder Mizzi began his record of agitation in the 1880s when he campaigned for a larger elected element in the legislative council, and opposed every attempt to diminish the status of Italian *vis-à-vis* English. He and his colleagues—notably Francesco Azzopardi and Mgr. Panzavecchio—were very successful, first in securing the introduction of representative government in 1887, then in bringing about its abolition in 1903, when Malta reverted—the first of a number of reversions—to a form of Crown Colony rule.[10] After the death of his father in 1905, Enrico Mizzi continued the good fight, entering the legislative council for the Mizzi stronghold of Gozo in 1916. The following year he was convicted of sedition, sentenced to a year's imprisonment, pardoned and forgiven, and continued undismayed to attack the administration through his newspaper, *Malta e sue Dependenzies de Partito Nationale*. Elected again to the new legislative council under the grant of (qualified) self-government in 1921,[11] he became the militant spirit of the Nationalist Party throughout the inter-war years, goading his more gentle leader Sir Ugo Mifsud into resisting the "anglicisation" of the courts, university and schools. By 1931 he was well-placed to direct the campaign, being Minister of Education during the second period of Nationalist rule.[12] The precise articles of his beliefs were never fully clear—he was after all a skilful politician as well as an intelligent lawyer—but the following quotation is a good example of the style and stance of this champion of the Italian cause. "The

L'Angleterre d'Outre-mer?

Italianity of Malta is, for the Maltese who are not renegades or ignorant, an axiomatic truth confirmed by all the moral and material elements which constitute the nationality of a people."[13] Rome, said Mizzi, had a double call: spiritual and lay. For the present, the Maltese owed "a dutiful loyalty to the British Crown", but it was to Italy not Britain that they should turn for their future safety and welfare. . . . His slogan, born of those years of opposition and taken up (as will be seen) in the debate over integration in the 1950s, was also characteristic: "Resistere, Resistere, Resistere!" When war was declared against Italy in 1940 Mizzi was again detained, deported to Uganda, and kept there until the end of hostilities. He returned ready still for action under the 1947 constitution, when Malta moved forward again to internal self-government, to become Leader of the Opposition to the Labour government under Dr. Paul Boffa until the 1950 elections when he led the Nationalist Party to victory only to die a few months later in office as Prime Minister.

Enrico Mizzi's opponent throughout these years was a no less redoubtable foe: Sir Gerald, later Lord, Strickland, Count della Catena, who had succeeded Sigismondo Savona as leader of the pro-English, *riformista* party. Strickland too was a lawyer, of English and Maltese descent,[14] an ardent Imperialist whose career was certainly no less extraordinary than that of Dr. Mizzi: originally an ally of Fortunato Mizzi in the campaign for representative government in the 1880s, then Chief Secretary in 1888 to the Government of Malta, Governor in 1902 of the Leeward Islands, Governor of Tasmania, Governor of Western Australia, and Governor of New South Wales. Returning to Malta in 1920 he took control of Dr. Augusto Bartolo's Constitutional Party, becoming leader of the Opposition in the Maltese Assembly from 1921 to 1927, member of Parliament also for Lancaster at Westminster 1924-7, Prime Minister of Malta 1927-1932,[15] and Leader of the elected majority in the Maltese Council of Government before he died in August, 1940. A man of many parts, each played honourably to the full; but not a man of tact or compromise. Sir Harry Luke, who was Lt. Governor of Malta in the 1930s and a great admirer of its peoples, described Strickland as "a robust Imperialist and a strenuous opponent of attempts to Italianise the Maltese.... But he was also combative and litigious. ...".[16] The Report of the Royal Commission of 1931 (which visited Malta to inquire into the working of the 1921 constitution) contained similar criticisms of the Prime Minister. "It is useless", said the Commissioners, "to disguise the opinion that Lord Strickland was a dominating and aggressive force, with a manner calculated to cause irritation and annoyance and with methods of attack which involved personal animosity on the part of many of those who were attacked, leading to a tendency for the whole Island to be divided into very embittered cliques."[17] In short, he was a pugnacious loyalist—loyal to the British Crown, and determined to use its local representative, the colonial government, in his struggle against the pro-Italian, Church-supported, Nationalists under Mizzi.[18]

As the conflict between the two sides moved from one crisis to another, widening from a local dispute

L'Angleterre d'Outre-mer?

over trade union representation in the Senate to a quarrel between Strickland and the Franciscan Conventual Order,[19] it brought in more powerful adversaries. What began as a political fight between party factions ended in an assertion of the rival claims of Church and State, Pope and Emperor, Rome and London. The Holy See despatched an Apostolic Delegate, Monsignor Pascal Robinson, to Valletta to uphold the privileges of the Church in Malta; Lord Strickland turned for help to His Majesty's Government in Britain. In 1930, the quarrel was brought into the open. A general election was due, and the Archbishop-Bishop of Malta, jointly with the Bishop of Gozo, issued a Pastoral Letter on 1st May, 1930 in language which was to be used for the next thirty years or more, first against the Constitutionalists and then against the Labour Party.[20] The electorate was warned that: "as Catholics:

(1) You may not, without committing a grave sin, vote for Lord Strickland and his candidates, or for all those, even of other parties, who in the past have helped and supported him in his fight against the rights and the discipline of the Church or who propose to help and support him in the coming elections.

(2) For even stronger reasons you may not present yourselves as candidates in the electoral lists proposed by Lord Strickland or by other parties who propose to support him in the coming elections.

(3) You are also solemnly bound in conscience in the present circumstances to take part in the elections and to vote for those persons who, by their attitude

in the past, offer a greater guarantee both for religious welfare and for social welfare.

In order, then, to prevent abuses in the administration and reception of the Sacraments, we remind our priests that they are strictly forbidden to administer the Sacraments to the obstinate who refuse to obey these our instructions."[21]

The British Government protested strongly to the Vatican (as indeed must have been expected) against the Church's "interferences with the freedom of electors in a British Colony to exercise their political judgment". The Cardinal Secretary of State (afterwards Pope Pius XII) rejected the protest, and put the blame on Lord Strickland and his attitude towards the Church in Malta. And there being no apparent way out of the impasse, the Governor of Malta, with the full approval of the Imperial Government, refused (May 1930) to allow the elections to be held, while retaining Lord Strickland's ministry in office "in a consultative capacity". It was in these circumstances, complicated still further by a legal conflict over the validity of certain local legislation, that the Askwith Commission arrived "to make full and diligent enquiry into the existing political situation in the island of Malta and to put forward recommendations as to the steps which are needed and should be taken for its amelioration".[22]

The primary recommendation of the Commissioners was that the 1921 constitution should be put to work again, in the somewhat forlorn hope that the conflict between Rome and London, Church and State, Nationalist and Constitutionalist parties, could be softened by local reforms. Accordingly, in March 1932,

L'Angleterre d'Outre-mer?

Lord Strickland resigned. In June, the elections which should have been held two years earlier took place, and again the Church in Malta was active though less openly than before. The Bishop actually withdrew a Pastoral Letter of the kind circulated in 1930. But there was little doubt of their hostility towards Strickland or of their support for the Nationalists who were returned to office with a sweeping majority under Sir Ugo Mifsud and Dr. Mizzi.[23] The latter now sought to restore the Italian language to its parity of status with English in the courts and primary schools: the colonial government pointed out that these were reserved matters under the constitution. When the Nationalist Ministry persisted, it found itself dismissed from office in November 1933, parliament dissolved, and the constitution suspended, the final blow being delivered by the Imperial government in 1936 when legislation was passed annulling the Letters Patent of 1921.[24] Malta returned once again—with modifications in 1939—to a colonial administrative form of rule until 1947 when "self-government" was once more restored.

What was the reason for these ups and downs, more akin to a constitutional game of snakes and ladders than to a controlled apprenticeship in the art of " responsible government "? Was it simply a problem of diarchy, of operating a constitution in which matters of Imperial concern tended to invade areas of local interest, and vice versa? The 1921 constitution was certainly a complicated one. There had been no lack of ingenuity on the part of the Imperial Government in its attempts to minimise its rule. Every device known to the Colonial Office had been introduced—a qualified franchise, an elected Assembly, a partly elected, partly appointed Senate, ministerial committees, a privy council, a local court of appeal, reserved powers for the Governor, and a careful division between Imperial and local matters: a splendid array of constitutional structures devised by legal officers and approved by the Maltese leaders themselves. Their operation, however, was a different matter, and the actual history of the islands, as we have seen, seemed evidence not of the adaptability of British rule but of its failure to find any formula which would meet the peculiar conditions of the "fortress and harbour colony". But when one looked below the surface of political life, the reason for this abrupt end to Maltese self-government could not be explained wholly in terms of a conflict between local and Imperial interests. There was the added complication of the bitter quarrel between rival factions among the educated Maltese themselves, each with its rank and file support: the pro-Italian Nationalists who had the organised power of the Church on their side, and the pro-Imperial Constitutionalists and their allies in the Labour Party among the large labour force in the dockyards of Valletta and the Three Cities. True, one might doubt whether the party faction fighting was really as deep-rooted as the leaders claimed it was. Despite the fact that the Maltese villager built his life around the Church festivals and the local "band club"—and had a passionate interest in "saints and fireworks"—he did not necessarily believe everything he heard from the pulpit. One might doubt, too, whether the dockyard workers who supported the Labour and Constitutionalist parties were really as

L'Angleterre d'Outre-mer?

interested in the niceties of the 1921 constitution as Lord Strickland said they were. Yet it remained true that, of those—Maltese men—entitled to vote, 95 per cent had done so in 1932, 86 per cent in 1927. What was to be done, therefore, when their leaders fell out?

The immediate answer of the colonial administration was simply to resume full control, and to justify the return of its rule by pointing to these divisions within local politics. There were certain advantages in the move back to Crown Colony government. It silenced the more abrasive and least loyal of the government's critics. It put an end to the Strickland-Mizzi quarrel.[25] And it secured the acquiescence of the Church whose primary concern was for the Catholic faith of its adherents, not for their civic or political rights. Hence the charge in later years that, by abolishing the 1921 constitution, colonial rule had restored "the material power of the clergy to its pristine glory".[26] But although the resumption of colonial control was an affront to the party leaders, it was probably of less consequence to the great majority of the population, whose loyalty to the British Crown was reinforced by the pride of place held by Malta in the long sea-linked chain of Imperial defence. It is difficult to recall in these post-imperial times the normality of colonial rule even as late as the 1930s.: it was not yet assumed that colonies were born to die. Nor was it at all clear that the dependent empire would evolve in a straight line of growth from colonial to Dominion status. Ceylon, to be sure, had moved forward in 1931, but very uncertainly, under a novel form of constitution. Newfoundland actually gave up its Dominion status in 1933. The times were full of peril for the small and weak, and although Imperial rule was autocratic it was also safe.

So at least it could be argued, and the colonial government settled down in the latter half of the 1930s to administer the islands after the fashion of what might today be called a modernising autocracy. "What e'er is best administered is best"? The period of Crown Colony rule after 1933 seemed almost to justify the precept, for the islands prospered. There were two principal causes. Although the Maltese have been prone to suffer in times of peace, and have suffered still more in times of actual conflict, they have usually thrived on the threat of war; and the brief span of years between the Abyssinian campaign and 1940, when the full weight of hostilities fell so cruelly on the islands, was a time of perpetual crisis. Rearmament in Britain had its parallel in the fortress colonies of Malta and Gibraltar. Expenditure increased and unemployment was greatly reduced. The second factor was the efficiency of the Maltese administration,[27] which applied itself to the practical tasks of local reform—road construction, hospital improvement, school building, the extension of the dockyards, the improvement of local agriculture—of which Malta stood in need. By 1939, the standard of living was higher than it had ever been: the national income per head was higher than that of Greece and not much below that of Italy.

These were substantial achievements. But the colonial administration was not content to govern alone. It went further. It borrowed a leaf from Lord Strickland's book and sought to strengthen the base of its rule by drawing on the local patriotism of the ordinary people. It attempted to offset the pro-Italian stand of the Nationalist Party by encouraging the growth of a rival Maltese nationalism among the people at large until the point was reached when—in Hancock's words —"British rule was appealing to the stunted Maltese nationalism of the masses against the cultural programmes which had been championed by the old nationalist party".[28] Such a policy was unusual. Most colonial governments have been anxious to curb rather than encourage nationalist emotions. But the circumstances surrounding local politics in Malta were also unusual. The collapse of the 1921 constitution had been brought about not by the assertion of an anti-colonial, popularly-based nationalism in Irish or Indian terms, but by the inability of the leaders of the two main parties to work together under an embryonic Westminster form of rule. Hence the argument of the colonial administration which was triple-edged: abolish the constitution, and thereby put an end to that limited conflict; justify the return of colonial rule by "good works"; and cultivate the affections of the ordinary Maltese through the "blending of an ancestral and Imperial patriotism".[29] Surely beneath the squabbles of the party leaders there was a basic unity among the Maltese people—for how else could they have survived as a people throughout the centuries of foreign rule? Suppose it could be encouraged? Might it not provide the basis both for British rule and for a new attempt in the future at self-government? It was at least worth a trial. And since the most obvious vehicle of nationalist feeling was language, the colonial administration turned to Maltese, "the humble language of the masses", and encouraged its use against Italian.

The story was not altogether new. Mizzi had fought half his life against such an encroachment, and was to spend a large part of his later years in the same struggle. Nor had he struggled in vain. The substitution of English for Italian even in the elementary schools (recommended by the Report of a Visiting Commissioner as early as 1880) was not fully adopted by the colonial administration until 1932, a little before the Nationalists took office. The pleas by Strickland for the inclusion of Maltese as a language of instruction at secondary school level had been ignored. But now the full weight and seal of official action was given to the task. Italian ceased to be the language of the law courts —thus ending the anomaly whereby jury members (but not the accused) had to be conversant with the Italian language—and was banished even from its high citadel in the law faculty of the university. The 1923 *pari passu* system of education, whereby Italian was preserved as a language of instruction in the secondary schools, was also swept aside. In brief: Italian lost its official status and English and Maltese were put in its place. The change was proclaimed by Imperial Letters Patent. "The English language as the official language of the British Empire, and the Maltese language as the language of the people of Malta, shall be the official languages of Malta." The accompanying despatch of the Secretary of State for the Colonies, Sir Philip Cunliffe-Lister, sought to justify the steps taken on the grounds of number: "only 15 per cent of the population can speak Italian. The general language of inter-

L'Angleterre d'Outre-mer?

course in the Island is Maltese which all Maltese of whatever class habitually speak; and English is far more widely used and understood in the Island than Italian." This "elevation of Maltese from the kitchen to the Courts",[30] understandably upset the leaders of the Nationalist Party. The Secretary of State was proclaimed an "assassin" who had vilely put to death "La grande e gloriosa lingua italiana . . . figlia primogenita della madre lingua latina" in favour "nella barbara lingua inglese e nel gergo Maltese".[31] But the new policy was carried out rigorously, with a careful attention to detail as well as to principle. "The spirit of the new call was expressed in the text books which the department of education produced: . . . books of Maltese history, told in the Maltese language, with the Union Jack stamped on the cover."[32] And the Nationalist Party—out of office despite its election victory—had to abide by the decision.

Such was the position in 1939 when these domestic quarrels were overborne by much larger conflicts. The tide of war swept once more over the islands in full recognition of their role as "one of the master keys of the British Empire",[33] and the effect was to justify many of the earlier hopes of the colonial government. The declaration of war first against Nazi Germany and then against Mussolini's Italy saw the growth not only of an intense local patriotism but a closer relationship with Britain. By 1941 Malta was besieged, under incessant attack from the air. And the attack was directed from the very country which the pro-Italian faction in the Nationalist Party had tried to uphold as the exemplar and guardian of the cultural traditions of the Maltese people as a whole. Like Britain, Malta stood embattled and alone, its plight almost desperate. The strength of its fortifications protected the islanders from very heavy casualties; but the daily bombardments, the shortage of food, the constant danger and threat of invasion, imposed a heavy burden. Under such conditions, the most courageous of nations will be sorely tried. But the Maltese are a stubborn, indomitable people. The siege strengthened both their national pride and loyalty to the Crown, and the government in Britain was quick to recognise their courage with the award of the George Cross by H.M. the King in April 1942: to "the Island Fortress of Malta to bear witness to a heroism and devotion that will long be famous in history". Maltese and British troops fought side by side in the island until by 1943 the worst was over. And it must have been with a lively satisfaction that the Maltese and British garrisons watched the arrival of the Italian fleet in the Grand Harbour on 10th September 1943, limping in to surrender unconditionally.

In that same year, 1943, the British government gave an undertaking to restore self-government at the end of war. Eventually they kept their promise, and Sir Harold MacMichael was appointed in 1946 to submit detailed recommendations in consultation with a specially convened National Assembly. There seemed little doubt now of the strong ties of affection between Malta and Britain. War had added its suffering, peace had brought victory to both countries, powerfully reinforcing the pre-war policy adopted by the colonial government. The final eclipse of the Italian element in the Nationalist party appeared certain. And on this

L'Angleterre d'Outre-mer?

assumption, the islands regained the measure of self-government they had lost in 1933. A new constitution,[34] introduced in September 1947, restored a diarchical form of rule. A unicameral legislative Assembly of 40 members, elected on an adult suffrage by proportional representation, was empowered to make laws "for the peace, order, and good government of Malta". A Cabinet of not more than eight ministers, including the Prime Minister, was responsible to the Assembly, while defence, civil aviation, currency, immigration, nationality—and "matters touching the public safety or defence of our dominions"—remained the responsibility of the Imperial Government in Malta, under the Governor.[35]

Less than ten years now separate the point reached in this first part of the story from the integration proposals of 1955-6. The pre-war controversies persisted—Enrico Mizzi had still to be Prime Minister—but they were beginning to take new forms: the Church in Malta versus the Malta Labour Party, rather than the Church and colonial state, Rome and London. The language question was all but dead, and when the 1947 constitution proclaimed Maltese and English to be the two official languages, there was no demur. Political alignments were also changing. At first sight they were kaleidoscopic—a bewildering minor universe of coalitions, realignments, new coalitions, old parties under new names, new parties with old labels: but by the mid-1950s the re-shaping of a well organised Labour Party had produced a similar consolidation on the right —the Nationalist Party, under the protective wing of the Church. The Maltese also managed to produce yet another remarkable politician, no less tenacious than Mizzi, no less pugnacious than Strickland: Dominic Mintoff, trained originally for the priesthood and now a young architect returned recently from Oxford, a Fabian Socialist, and a member of the Malta Labour Party who had been elected to the interim Council of Government in 1945.

All that remains therefore in these concluding pages is to set down plainly the chronicle of events which brought Mintoff to power in 1955. They began with the first post-war elections under the new constitution and the arrival in office of the Labour Party under Dr. Paul Boffa. In 1949 Mintoff quarrelled with his leader, whom he accused not only of neglecting the interests of the dockyard workers, nearly 1,500 of whom were to be discharged in the forthcoming financial year, but of failing to secure for the islands a proper share of "Marshall Aid". The crisis was dramatic, and in the light of later events ominous. It included Mintoff's "London ultimatum" to the British Government (against Boffa's wishes) which declared that: "Before the end of August, the British Government should consent to Malta's receiving a direct share of Marshall Aid. Failing this outcome, the Malta government would ask the people in a national referendum whether they wish to stay in the Commonwealth or throw in their lot with the United States. . . ." The ultimatum was contained in a letter to the Secretary of State for the Colonies from Mintoff and the Malta Commissioner in London, Edward Ellul, and was repudiated by Boffa in August 1949, whereupon Mintoff resigned as deputy prime minister and Minister for

L'Angleterre d'Outre-mer?

Public Works. By October, however, he had ousted Boffa as leader of the Labour movement, splitting the rank and file into a majority and minority party. The result was that the Nationalists took office after the 1950 election, first as a minority government under Mizzi, then in 1951 and 1953 under Dr. Giorgio Borg Olivier in alliance with a "Malta Workers' Party" (brought together by Boffa), until they too were defeated early in 1955. The full run of elections between 1947 and 1955 was as follows:

Prime Minister	Parties and Seats					
	Nat.	MLP	MWP	DAP	Const.	Others
1947 Boffa	7	24	—	4	—	5
1950 Mizzi	12	11	11	1	4	1
1951 Borg Olivier	15	14	7	—	4	0
1953 Borg Olivier	18	19	3	—	0	0
1955 Mintoff	17	23	—	—	0	0

Note: (a) The Constitutionalist Party was dissolved by Roger Strickland early in 1946, revived by Professor Galea in 1950 and reconstituted by Miss Mabel Strickland in October 1953 as the Progressive Constitutional Party.

(b) DAP=the Democratic Action Party, a brief revival of the 1921-6 *Unione Politica* tending to represent the professional class in Valletta and Sliema.

So Mintoff became Prime Minister in February 1955 and almost immediately put forward certain proposals for integration which the Malta Labour Party had begun to advocate in the 1950-53 elections. The British Government under Sir Anthony Eden was understandably cautious in its reply but not at all negative. It followed a time-honoured practice, and convened a Round Table Conference (representative of all parties in Britain) whose members saw as their "primary task" the need "to decide how far the proposals for closer association, and, in particular, those put forward by the Maltese Government are consonant with the interests and requirements of both the United Kingdom and Malta, and with the responsibilities of the Imperial Parliament".[36] The membership was of high standing: Lord Kilmuir as chairman, C. R. Attlee, Clement Davies, Walter Elliott, Aneurin Bevan, Chuter Ede, James Griffiths, Lord Listowel, W. P. Spens, Lord Perth, Kenneth Pickthorn, John MacKay, W. Atkins, Julian Amery, R. H. S. Crossman, Douglas Houghton and Richard Wood. They met first in London and then in Malta, their Report appeared in December, and concluded that "representation at Westminster [was] practicable and reasonable". It was for the Maltese people "to determine and to demonstrate clearly and unmistakably whether the proposals of the Maltese Government [for representation at Westminster] do indeed correspond to their own wishes". If they did, the Conference was prepared to "recommend . . . acceptance by Her Majesty's Government in the United Kingdom and by the Parliament at Westminster" of the proposal that there should be not less than three Maltese representatives in the House of Commons.[37]

PART II

The 1956 Referendum

THERE it was: a clear agreement apparently between the two sides. Mintoff wanted it, Lord Kilmuir's conference agreed to it. All that remained, it seemed, was to put the proposition before the Maltese people (although not before the British electorate) and await the result. How were these proposals for closer association arrived at? And what was intended by them? The British side can be left for inquiry to the third section of this monograph since their apparent readiness to take the Maltese islands into their embrace is best discussed in terms of the changes in British policy towards the Commonwealth and its dwindling colonial empire. The Malta side on the other hand needs further comment since it was on the outcome of the wishes of "the Maltese people themselves" that the proposals were to stand or fall.

What have we learnt so far? That the Maltese hold strongly to the belief that they are a "free" people who came voluntarily under the British Crown. They are also a Catholic nation, many of whom are fiercely anti-clerical. So much is clear from the previous section. A large part of that anti-clericalism had been located in the Constitutionalist Party under Strickland,

and had found a second home in the Labour Party under Mintoff. Their opponents were political allies of the Church to which they looked for electoral support. They were "Nationalists", a somewhat misleading appellation in the past when many of their leaders had professed an uncritical admiration for the language and culture of the neighbouring mainland; but by 1955 the Italian element in the Nationalist Party was greatly diminished partly as a result of the war, partly also because of the policies adopted by the colonial administration before the war. A new generation of local leaders had come out of the primary, secondary and university schools to whom the Maltese language and Maltese history were no longer subordinate elements in a wider and superior Italian culture but natural vehicles of a fierce local patriotism: the effect was particularly noticeable on the Nationalist Party whose focus was now more "Malta-centred". There were other contributory causes. Mussolini was dead, Italy an ally, Malta a NATO base, Britain an imperial power beginning to retreat: even Mizzi had been accepted as Prime Minister by the colonial administration once the language question had ceased to be a contentious issue.

Thus the primary issue in the 1950s was raised not by the Nationalists but by the Labour Party—whether Mintoff and his supporters could carry Malta all the way into Westminster. It was an imaginative proposal which might well have gladdened the heart of Lord Strickland although not (as we shall discover) that of his daughter. And there were good grounds for supposing that it might be possible. The heroism of the war, and a generous grant-in-aid by Britain to the war-

The 1956 Referendum

stricken islands, had brought the two countries close together. The Round Table Conference, which commended the proposals, put great emphasis on "the traditions which Malta has chosen to share with us. She voluntarily came under the British Crown 150 years ago and continued to accept, with the prestige and material benefits of being a strong-hold in the Mediterranean, the difficulties of an island Fortress economy. She has been a tower of strength to the causes which the British and Maltese people both believe to be those of a civilisation of which Malta has been again and again a bastion. The two world wars of this century have set their seal on Britain and Malta standing together." Now in 1955 that close relationship had suddenly blossomed into proposals for a political union of the two peoples. If it was an unusual imperial venture for Britain it was an even more unusual response to British rule on the part of a British colony.

So much by way of summary of what has already been said. But we must not lose sight of what was still a basic dilemma of the Maltese islands—their location. In the mid-1950s Malta remained a "fortress colony", part of the chain of imperial defence from Gibraltar to Aden and the Far East, and heavily dependent on British defence expenditure. The Maltese were "faced with an immensely difficult problem" being "wholly dependent on one industry, defence,"[1] and the employment figures alone told their story. By 1957 the population of working age, men and women, numbered 185,686: those actually in employment were 89,200. But whereas in the mid-nineteenth century, defence and administrative requirements absorbed only 2 per cent of the labour force, the proportion had increased to 18 per cent by 1931 and to over 27 per cent in 1957. Thereafter, the number employed in the great naval dockyard and its ancillary services declined rapidly because of the transfer of the yards from Admiralty control and their conversion to commercial use. But, in the mid-1950s, independence was ruled out because of an imperial interest which it was also clearly to the advantage of the Maltese to serve. The Round Table Conference was categorical in its rejection of the transfer of sovereignty. The "road to full self-government", it declared, "is blocked, in that Parliament at Westminster must, in order to maintain the defences of Malta and the facilities necessary to enable it to fulfil its role as one of the principal Commonwealth and NATO bases in the Mediterranean, exercise overriding powers in Malta in the fields of defence and foreign affairs". Somehow, therefore, the just demand of the Maltese for an end to their colonial status needed to be reconciled with their practical dependence on the power which alone could determine the extent of their dependence.

How was it to be done? Various schemes, including integration with Britain, had already been suggested in an attempt to soften, and if possible disguise, the inequality of status between the British and Maltese islands. Miss Mabel Strickland who was—is happily still—indefatigable in her efforts to guard the interests of her fellow islanders, had raised the question of integration—suggesting that Malta might become a "county"—as early as 1943 in her paper the *Times of Malta*.[2] The Malta Labour Party manifestoes for the

The 1956 Referendum

1950, 1951 and 1953 elections had talked of the possibility of a "gradual union" and the "integration" of Malta with the United Kingdom over a twenty year period. These were tentative explorations of the problem, designed as much to find a way round the impasse between imperial interests and local rights as having a detailed end in view. But if they were little more than gestures in the direction of a closer association between Britain and Malta at least they had the merit of boldness. The Nationalist alternative was more cautious—and simply led into the impasse. In June 1953, Dr. Borg Olivier submitted a memorandum to John Hopkins, Minister of State for Colonial Affairs, in which it was requested that Malta be given a form of qualified Dominion status under the Commonwealth Relations Office. The argument was used—it was employed again during the debate over integration—that the George Cross Island was "unique" both in its capacity for self-government and in its inability to achieve it. "Imperial interests have so far been involved to deny to the Maltese people the full measure of self-government to which, by their history and traditions, by the unique manner in which they came under protection, by the magnitude of their contributions to the common good and by their fitness to govern their own affairs they are justly entitled."[3] They ought not therefore to be classified as a dependency but as a Self-Governing Colony, like Rhodesia, under the Dominions Office although even that, if granted, was not "*per se* an adequate satisfaction of the constitutional ideals and aspirations of the Maltese people".

Such was the substance of the Nationalist argument

and the Secretary of State had replied via the Governor Sir Gerald Creasy. Her Majesty's Government was willing to respond in principle but there was the problem of "imperial interests". "I must say in all frankness that it seems to us that the position of Malta as a Fortress (the source of her livelihood) must unavoidably entail some constitutional restrictions on full self-government in the field of Defence and External Affairs. On account of this and of her relative size and disabilities imposed by her lack of natural resources, Malta is not . . . eligible to be considered for full independent membership of the Commonwealth." There was, however, an alternative possibility. Her Majesty's Government was willing "to transfer responsibility for handling business relating to Malta . . . to the Home Secretary who is the Secretary of State immediately concerned as the Queen's Minister in relation to the United Kingdom and neighbouring Isles. . . . Malta would be under the authority of the Queen in Council with the Home Secretary as the responsible Minister."[4]

Here was a possible step towards integration although the Home Office clearly considered Malta to be an outlying group of islands more like the Isle of Man and the Channel Islands than the Orkneys and the Isle of Wight: that is, under the Crown but not represented in the parliament at Westminster. The Nationalists were unimpressed. The suggestion smacked too much of name changing, and did nothing to alter the fundamental problem of diarchy in terms of imperial and domestic interests. An interim statement in November 1953 declared that "prima facie" the suggestion

The 1956 Referendum

seemed "likely to retard rather than promote the constitutional advancement of these islands".[5] It was agreed however—a year later—to hold joint talks in London. Then a further general election intervened, and the Labour Party was elected to office with twenty-three of the forty seats on a specific programme of integration with Britain. Mintoff travelled to London, declared himself in favour of "full integration", and talks were held in June-July 1955 between the British government and representatives of the Malta Labour and Nationalist parties. Such was the immediate background to the Round Table meeting.

How serious was Mintoff in his bid for integration? Serious enough at least to be taken seriously by H.M. Government in London. There were of course accusations both in Malta and Britain that Mintoff's prime motive was financial—that like Mrs. Todgers' embracing of the Miss Pecksniffs "there was affection beaming in one eye and calculation shining out of the other" —but that was not inconsistent with the wish for a closer constitutional relationship between Malta and Britain: indeed, it could be argued that integration was a necessary condition of continued economic help. The basis of the Labour Party in Valletta and the Three Cities was the large number of dockyard workers whose primary concern after 1945 was to ward off the effect of any reduction in British defence expenditure. Mintoff's quarrel with Boffa in 1949 had been over the questions of financial aid by Britain, and integration held out the hope not only of a safeguard against economic hardship but of immediate and direct benefits: "£9 a week". Little wonder, therefore, that Mintoff's proposals were popular among his Labour Party followers.

But Mintoff also hoped to put an end to the colonial status of the Maltese islands; and although at first sight the proposals put forward retained the notion of diarchy between Imperial and domestic matters, they did so within the wider context of representation at the centre and a clearer autonomy at home. Mintoff and his colleagues (it was said) had looked at the pattern of representation in Paris of the French-speaking colonies as well as the position of Hawaii and Puerto Rico *vis-à-vis* Washington; but they wanted not only a direct voice and vote at Westminster but greater control over local Maltese affairs.[6] So it came about that in successive elections between 1950 and 1953 they began to argue the case for representation at Westminster and devolution in Valletta, which they described as "integration". Unless therefore an extraordinary measure of cunning is attributed to Mintoff, whereby he advocated integration, knowing first that it would fail, and then that the way would be opened somehow, at some time in the future, to independence —and one had only to state the proposition in these terms to see how implausible it was in 1956—there is no reason to doubt the seriousness of the request made by the Malta Labour Government to the Conservative administration under Eden.

We can turn now to the recommendations themselves. In broad terms they were as follows. Firstly, the British Government should retain a final responsibility for foreign relations, defence and, at a later date when

The 1956 Referendum

the economy of Malta had moved towards "parity" with that of the United Kingdom, direct taxation. Secondly, the relationship between the Maltese and British parliaments needed to be redefined in the interests of a greater degree of autonomy on the part of the Maltese parliament. There would be no interference by Westminster in the powers of the Maltese parliament—a "rule of construction", in familiar Commonwealth guise, which would be established not in law but by convention. Thirdly, the position and rights of the Church in Malta should not be diminished. Fourthly, "communication" between Valletta and London would be improved in terms of "consultation and cooperation".[7] Fifthly, there was need still for Britain to continue to help the islands to reach a higher standard of living and—at some future point in time—parity with the United Kingdom. Sixthly, there should be not fewer than three Maltese representatives (elected in accordance with United Kingdom law) in the House of Commons, a proposal which was linked to the first proposition of the Report since it was precisely because of the possibility of conflict between the two countries over defence and external affairs that the need arose for a Maltese voice to be heard on such matters at Westminster itself.

These broad items of agreement were then submitted to the electorate in Malta, Gozo, and Comino at a referendum on February 11th and 12th, 1956 (a Saturday and Sunday) in the wind and rain of a Maltese winter. By early morning on the 14th the vote was counted: 74 per cent in favour, 22 per cent against, and Mintoff announced that he was very satisfied. A

Malta and the End of Empire

statement issued from the Auberge d'Aragon[8] began:

"I am delighted at the rock steady support of the Malta Labour government's plea of closer union with Britain for the social and economic progress of Malta . . ."

On 25th March the British government accepted the principle of integration, and announced that a Malta Bill would be introduced along the lines of the Round Table Conference recommendations. Meanwhile, agreement was sought on the substance of what was involved in the enlargement of the United Kingdom to include the Maltese islands, a principal aim being that of "economic equivalence"; that is, the attainment within twelve to fifteen years of a standard of living in Malta comparable with that in Britain—a remarkable declaration of intent under which the British government agreed to provide £25 million over five years towards the financing of a new Development Plan, plus a minimum of £1 million a year for the improvement of social services in the islands.

At this point we must look more closely at the Maltese end of the bargaining. And if, having done so, the reader feels that he has been misled, the fault is not entirely the writer's. The sequence of events has been set down as they took place, and the plain fact of the matter is that both the British government and the Labour Party under Mintoff acted together during the post-referendum period with an air of almost calculated self-deception by taking the voting results at their face value, as given earlier in this section: 74 per cent in favour, 22 per cent against. But let us look at the votes in greater detail:

The 1956 Referendum

(1) Electorate	152,823	
(2) Voters	90,343	59%
(3) For Integration	67,607	74% of (2), 44% of (1)
(4) Against Integration	20,177	22% of (2) ⎫ 85,216
(5) Spoiled Votes	2,559	4% of (2) ⎬ =56%
(6) Non-Voters	62,480	— ⎭ of (1)

It could be argued that less than half the electorate had voted for integration and that the Labour Party had actually lost support, its share of the poll—despite an increase in the electorate[9]—falling by nearly a thousand votes since the 1955 election. Borg Olivier was quick to make the point. Mr. Mintoff, he said, had talked at the Round Table Conference in terms of having 75 per cent of the people with him: but the referendum showed otherwise. "The Nationalists obeyed their leaders' instructions to oppose both the Referendum and the Integration proposals by boycotting the poll. The result of the Referendum is an expression of the people's lack of enthusiasm in, let alone enthusiasm for, integration. The plan should be dropped forthwith."[10] The debate on 17th February in the Malta parliament on a Motion for the Adjournment—the first to be held on integration—was clamorous. When the prime minister announced that the results of the referendum were a source of the greatest satisfaction to the government, there were shouts of "Resign, resign! Keep your word." The Prime Minister continued:

Mintoff: The Government party was not fighting the opposition parties at the Referendum. The Government said they would resign if they did not secure a majority at the Referendum.

—Uproar—

Mintoff (cont.d): If the Government had been fighting only the two opposing political parties they would have polled 100,000 votes.

—Uproar—

The Speaker then suspended Dr. G. M. Camilleri (Nat.) from the House for five minutes, and Mintoff continued with an attack on the Church:

Mintoff: . . . Until that same day absolution was being refused to penitents in Gozo if they favoured Integration. . . . The British Government would now consider the Referendum result . . .

—Uproar—The Strangers' Gallery was cleared amidst shouts of "Thieves", "Liars", etc.

Mintoff: The Government would do its best to remove existing doubts . . . The Government was ready to resume the responsibility of Government as cheerfully as before the Referendum. Integration would come into effect.

What had happened? Mintoff tried to draw a distinction between party conflict and the opposition of the Church authorities. The Nationalist Party (he argued) was against integration simply because of party politics. The opposition of the Church was more serious but less permanent, being based on a misunderstanding of the likely effect of integration. Had there been "no clash of loyalties over the [question of] guarantees to the Church", said Mintoff, there would have been "much less anxiety among the population in general" and a correspondingly smaller vote against the

The 1956 Referendum

proposals. The argument was plausible—as far as it went; but it did not go very far. The hostility of the Church was indeed critical: but it was also fundamental and there seemed little reason to suppose that it could be assuaged, or that the alliance of Church hierarchy and Nationalist leadership would be broken as long as Mintoff and the Labour party remained in office.

The remarkable feature of the referendum was the large number who abstained, primarily at the instigation of the Church, supported by the Nationalist Party. To explain the run of these votes we must turn aside a little from the main theme and try to look in on the political debate which took place during the weeks preceding the referendum.

We might begin with the Labour Party. Its main emphasis, strongly endorsed by the General Workers Union, was on the direct economic advantages to be gained from integration. The point was made by Mintoff early in February 1955 in an issue of the party paper *The Knight*: "Let me take a standard example of a married man with a wife and three children to support. His average weekly wage in Malta today is about £5; after the full impact of integration, in say five years time, his average wage will be £9 a week."[11] The argument was repeated again and again during the actual campaign for a "yes vote" both by the Labour Party and the G.W.U. A joint broadcast by Mintoff and Mr. R. G. Miller of the Workers Union on 9 February, 1956 emphasised that "integration hinged on three conditions" of which the first was that it would lead to "an improvement in local standards of living

Malta and the End of Empire

and the economic development of the island", including the development of its "industrial potential with British help until the local standard is raised to reach that of the United Kingdom". That was the prime consideration, the second being "full autonomy except for defence and foreign affairs", and the third "representation at Westminster". The full spread of argument, put by the Labour Party at rallies, meetings, and in the press, appeared in an issue of the *Bulletin* as early as 14th January, 1956 under the heading, "Straight Questions and Straight Replies", and it may be useful to reproduce them here in a shortened form.

STRAIGHT QUESTIONS AND STRAIGHT REPLIES

by the Scarlet Pimpernel

When the Referendum will be held the people of Malta and Gozo will be asked to answer very straight questions. Here they are one by one:

Are you to vote in favour of Malta M.P.s at Westminster? ... I hope you agree with me that Maltese M.P.'s at the House of Commons can attract attention to our complaints. Of course, they can never be strong enough to obtain a favourable decision or reverse an unfavourable one by a majority vote. But they can always state the facts on our behalf, and reasonable men can be trusted to see a point when there is one.

The next question: *Are you in favour of Westminster being solely responsible for Defence and Foreign Affairs and, eventually, Direct Taxation of the Maltese?* ... We live in a small world surrounded by politically ambitious and aggressive countries ... So our defence and

The 1956 Referendum

foreign relations must continue to remain the concern of Westminster. The second part of the question regards direct taxation. That, naturally, will be subject to the principle of relativity as regards salaries, wages and the quantity and quality of social services. But if we get social services to be paid for us by the British taxpayer, it is only right that we suffer direct taxation only to the extent of the benefits and social advantages received in return ...

The next question: *Are you in favour of U.K. Government's confirming the assurance they have already given in regard to religious matters?* The answer is not only an unequivocal yes, but also a "yes" that will demand constitutionally fool proof guarantees.

The next question: *Are you in favour of the abolition of Diarchy and establishment of consultative machinery between Malta and Britain?* I think that this is not only an inevitable corollary of the whole situation, but meets also a general consensus of all the political parties.

The next question: *Are you in favour of the gradual raising of the standard of living, and particularly social services for the people of these Islands?* The answer is an emphatic "yes". This is the raison d'être of the proposed constitutional changes.

The questions aim at obtaining a popular mandate not only in favour of a change in the constitutional status of Malta as an integral member of the United Kingdom, but also the assurance of common advantages and common responsibilities to be shared with inhabitants of the United Kingdom, direct taxation remaining proportionate to the scale of salaries and wages prevailing in the island.

The strength of the Labour Party was derived not only from its anti-clericalism but from its appeal to the "common man".[12] It reached down into the villages:[13] it was a "mass party", organised hierarchically, but with a broad popular base particularly among the dockworkers in the Three Cities, and it had little difficulty in carrying its supporters along with the leaders in their proposals for integration. Its ally—equal in status and in no way subordinate to the party—was the powerful General Workers Union, by far the biggest of the thirty or more employees' associations.[14] And throughout 1955 and the early months of 1956 the G.W.U. supported the arguments put forward by Mintoff—as in the questions and answers supplied by the "Scarlet Pimpernel"—against mounting opposition both from the Nationalist and Constitutionalist parties and the Church.

The Nationalist party opposed integration. Being much less dependent for its support on the unions and the dockyard workers, the party had a correspondingly smaller interest in the economic benefits which, it was argued, would follow from integration. Yet it did not oppose the Round Table Report directly. It called upon its members to boycott the referendum on the grounds that the guarantees promised to the Church had not been properly spelt out. The party's call for a boycott also reflected a basic uncertainty in the Nationalists' position since its alternative to integration was at best imprecise. The party had proposed to the Round Table Conference that "Malta should ultimately achieve a new form of full self-government within the Commonwealth in which it would be autonomous in its relations with the United Kingdom but not with the Commonwealth and foreign countries. Defence and Com-

The 1956 Referendum

monwealth and Foreign Affairs would be the joint responsibility of the United Kingdom and Malta and would be governed by agreements to be made between the two governments". But it was not easy to be sure what was meant by such a programme. It was broad enough to conceal a wide range of opinion within the party itself, so wide indeed that by 1958 a right wing section had detached itself from Dr. Borg Olivier's leadership. Listen to Dr. Herbert Ganado of the future Democratic Nationalist Party and a familiar echo is heard. It is that of Enrico Mizzi to whose memory fulsome tribute was paid. "Enrico Mizzi has left us a message, the watchword of a lifetime: 'Resistere, Resistere, Resistere'. Resistance unto death. This must be the holy ideal and guiding inspiration of Maltese youth in its struggle against the present desperate effort to prostitute our faith, adulterate our nationality and corrupt our Freedom by integrating Malta with the United Kingdom."[15] In more moderate language, the Nationalist Party tried to justify its call for a boycott not only on the grounds that the Labour Party had deceived the Maltese people, in asking them to vote before the details of the proposals were known, but because integration was incompatible with the "unfettered local autonomy promised in the Labour Party's manifesto".[16] The main burden of its case lay in the argument that British and Maltese interests were so close that the two governments could act in harmony in defence and national affairs—provided each was a free agent. "We reiterate at the risk of pedantry that in such matters the two governments can, nay, must reach an agreement, but the Maltese people will never accept a *diktat* . . . So we ask, Why integration? Why should we deliver ourselves in perpetuity and renounce our sacred rights to be free in our country? Borg Olivier was right when he said: "I shall be serving the British Commonwealth better if I serve my country best."

The Nationalist Party was now unmistakably nationalist, although in trying to gauge its opposition towards integration one must allow for a large measure of direct hostility towards Mintoff and the Labour Party. The tone of that hostility can be recorded by quoting once again from *The Bulletin*, a week later in time:

DISHONEST REPLIES TO MISLEADING QUESTIONS

By Sempronius

The dishonest and misleading questions put by Scarlet Pimpernel in his article of last Saturday are even more so than the proposals published by the Socialist Government in the Government Gazette in terms of the Referendum Act.

His answers remind one of the replies usually expected by a doped "self-admitting" criminal behind the Iron Curtain or the easy and simple arguments put out by Moscow Radio in defence of Russian democracy.

Are you to vote in favour of Malta M.P.s at Westminster? An honest and unselfish answer would be NO, for three M.P.s can never have the same weight *vis-à-vis* the U.K. Government as a local autonomous Parliament could have.

Are you in favour of Westminster being solely responsible for Defence and Foreign Affairs and, eventually, Direct Taxation of the Maltese? Certainly NOT . . . we prefer discussing defence and foreign affairs as an autonomous

The 1956 Referendum

Government, even if in our mutual interests we will have to recognise, out of our own free will, that the other equal partner is right in his assertions. With regard to direct taxation we do not want to lose the power of the purse, for without that power our pseudo-Parliament would become a mockery . . .

Are you in favour of the Maltese Parliament being in possession of powers excluding those of Defence, Foreign Relations and, eventually, Direct Taxation of the Maltese? Definitely NOT, for I wish to see our Parliament enjoying more powers than it has now and not less . . .

Are you in favour of the U.K. Government's confirming the assurance they have already given in regard to religious matters? I would first have preferred to examine and study the extent and full implications of this assurance. . . . With regard to the Church, the over-riding powers of Westminster are bound to diminish its influence, in the course of time, in the educational field; also because the social aspect of life of the British people is becoming every day more and more atheist.

Are you in favour of the abolition of Diarchy and establishment of consultative machinery between Malta and Britain? If for Imperial interests no more liberal constitution is available to us than the 1947 one, I would rather have the status quo . . .

Are you in favour of the gradual raising of the standard of living, and particularly social services for the people of these islands? Certainly, but not under the menace of Integration . . .

I challenge Scarlet Pimpernel and Mr. Mintoff himself to prove to me by documentary evidence, by quoting from the Report, that the Maltese will be deprived the economic aid recommended in the Report, and in the light of the

July agreement, were they to refuse to send representatives to Westminster. If they do I will join them in voting for Integration. If they don't, they are in bad faith...

The Nationalist Party had climbed slowly back in popular favour since the war,[17] always retaining its appeal among the lawyers and notaries of Sliema and Valletta, but drawing on a wider following as the party of the Church—strong wherever the parish priest was strong, particularly among the smaller villages of Malta and the still largely rural population of Gozo. The party leader, Borg Olivier, had none of the wild extravagance of Enrico Mizzi; nor could he rival Dom Mintoff in public appeal. But if, in the popular view, he lacked "charisma", he was by no means unskilful as a politician: he was sensible, moderate, cautious, reliable, patient—qualities which were all the more evident—and, to many, admirably so—when set against the wayward brilliance of his Labour opponent. He held the party steady, against not only the Labour and Constitutionalist parties, but the extremist elements among his own followers who sought, still, to drag the party back into the quarrels and savage invective of the pre-war years. True, he was strongly opposed to the Round Table's recommendations; and he insisted that the party should boycott the referendum: but he was also prepared to resist attempts to sour Anglo/Maltese relations in general on the particular and single issue of integration.[18]

The Progressive Constitutionalist Party was also against integration. Less abusive, more positive, but much fewer in number than the Nationalists, Miss Strickland's party called upon the electorate to "vote

The 1956 Referendum

No in order to defend the rights of the Church and of the Maltese Nation against the Labour plan of integration". Gone was the old quarrel between the Church authorities and Lord Strickland's Constitutionalist Party. In a broadcast on 7th February Miss Mabel Strickland supported the Archbishop's plea that the referendum should be postponed to allow time for the formulation of guarantees to protect the Church. If the referendum was held, the electorate should vote "No". The party had "no wish to let the Socialists absorb us in their parliament", nor to allow a Protestant ascendancy to diminish the control of the Church over education and marriage.[19] Miss Strickland actually sought a judgment of the courts that the Governor had acted *ultra vires* in December 1955 in signing the Warrant for the holding of a referendum, but lost her case before the Appeal Court in January 1956. In her evidence to the Round Table Conference, and in many issues of the *Times of Malta,* Miss Strickland argued against integration in support of a greater autonomy for the island (possibly under a Ministry for Maltese Affairs):

I personally am convinced that the indirect rule of the House of Commons would be almost worse than that of the Colonial Office. You well know what Cornwall thinks of the central Government . . . Malta is 1,500 miles away . . . We do not want our 150 years of real loyalty upset by this idea. Of course it might have been a different conception if you had an overseas parliament of all the colonies . . . but all that was jettisoned by the Statute of Westminster . . . If we want to go into the Parliament of Westminster let us get elected by the people of the United Kingdom as my father was. If any of you want

Malta and the End of Empire

to come into our Parliament, come and stand in Malta. You will have to learn Maltese first . . .[20]

The 20,000 and more who voted "No" in 1956 undoubtedly included supporters of the PCP, but by far the greater number of them must also have thought that they were following the injunction of the Church which succeeded in making its dislike of integration very plain without categorically directing its congregation to vote against the proposals rather than to abstain from voting. Here indeed was the chief opponent of the Labour Party, all the more powerful because of its ambiguities; and in a characteristic outburst Mintoff complained that "the fight was no longer between his Party and the Nationalist and Ghost parties but between his party and all those who exploited religion because they agreed with the Italians".[21] It is time therefore to turn not to Rome or Italy but to the Roman Church in Malta and the part played by the ecclesiastical hierarchy under yet another remarkable Maltese leader: Monsignor Michael Gonzi, a foundation member of the Labour Party in 1920, Bishop of Gozo in 1924, a fierce opponent of the Constitutional Party during the inter-war years (when the Labour Party moved towards a working alliance with Strickland), and implacably opposed to Mintoff and the 1955 Labour government.

Following publication of the Report of the Round Table Conference, His Grace the Metropolitan Archbishop of Malta and His Lordship the Bishop of Gozo issued a Pastoral Letter from the Archiepiscopal curia. It was to be read in all churches on Sunday, 22nd

The 1956 Referendum

January. The main burden of the Letter concerned the question of guarantees for the autonomy of the Church. What would happen if Westminster (with its three Maltese members) enacted legislation which was inimical to the Church? "We think that the danger can only be eliminated if, in the document embodying the form of the new constitution or in the documents and official declarations accompanying the constitution, the observance of the recommendations of the Conference be guaranteed for the future." There was no readiness here to trust to conventions. On the contrary: there was a profound distrust of Mintoff and the Labour Party. " We should not be satisfied", said the Letter, "simply with the good intentions of persons who are with us today." Nor should one lose sight of the fact "that there are great differences between Britain and Malta. While in Britain people of diverse religions are to be found, Malta is wholly Catholic and the people of Malta wish to remain faithful to the Catholic traditions inherited from our forefathers".

Early in February, the Archbishop wrote to the Governor asking that a provision be inserted in any future Integration Act along lines of paragraph 79 in the Round Table Report, as follows:

Whereas the Roman Catholic religion is the religion of Malta and its Dependencies, nothing shall be done by way either by legislation or administration which shall diminish or detract from the prerogatives as now enjoyed by, or from the present position of, the Roman Catholic Church in Malta in all matters in which the Church is directly concerned, and in particular as regards the marriage laws relating to family life and education.

Thus the "guarantee clause" became the main ground of difference not only between the Malta government and the Church but between the Labour Party and all its opponents including the Nationalist and Constitutionalist parties. The Archbishop insisted that, until an assurance was given by the British Government that such a guarantee would be given, the referendum should be postponed.

The Secretary of State did his best to assure His Lordship. When asked by James Griffiths about the need for such a guarantee, Lennox Boyd replied:

I can ... assure the House that Her Majesty's Government will not commend to Parliament any proposals which run counter to the assurances given to the Archbishop of Malta by representatives of the Round Table Conference as set out in paragraph 79 of its Report.[22]

It was a clear, plain statement. Nevertheless it failed, not only because the Church was opposed under almost any terms to the integration of Catholic Malta with a Protestant England, but because of the profound distrust with which it viewed any action taken by Mintoff. And Mintoff for his part declared that he saw no need at this stage for such guarantees. They could come later. The Archbishop (he said) had shifted his position from his earlier position, and it was too late to protest. The referendum would go forward. The Labour Party "drew its inspiration from the teaching of Christ as interpreted by the Church" but it also wished "to free Malta from the state of a subservient colony" and the electorate should vote "yes".

If the dispute between the Curia and Mintoff's government was barbed, the quarrel at lower level was often venomous, particularly when it brought in outside comment. When a correspondent in the London *Daily Herald* argued that "integration will mean the emancipation of Malta and Gozo from the undue influence of the Archbishop", the Maltese paper *The Faith*[23] seized on the words as part of a general review of the Round Table proposals. It was "symptomatic" of what might follow integration. "The plea that the Maltese would not make use of divorce laws were they to be applied to Malta, that birth limitation by artificial means should be indirectly encouraged, that secular literature should have free-handed circulation in Malta, and that police notices for decency at the beaches should be removed—all these and others are also symptoms that a very serious situation is in the budding." As the campaign hotted up, the language of debate became inflamed. A resolution was adopted by the numerous Church associations—Catholic Action,[24] Museum,[25] Legion of Mary, Holy Name Society, Young Christian Workers, Marian Congregations, Catholic Women's League and the Knights of Columbus—declaring that "from the pastoral Letter of the Bishops of Malta and Gozo, as well as from the letter sent by the Vatican to the Prime Minister, it clearly appears that if the Integration proposals were to be accepted without the guarantees which the Church demands, the Faith and the Catholic morals in Malta would be endangered!" They appealed to the people "not to vote in favour of Integration in the forthcoming referendum unless the Church declares herself to be satisfied with

Malta and the End of Empire

the constitutional guarantees which she has asked for and has not been granted".

As the date of the referendum drew near, the Church tried hard to clarify its position without actually saying what it meant. The first announcement came from Gozo in a statement by the Very Reverend Mgr. Archpriest Michael Cefai, president of the Council of Parish Priests of the Diocese of Gozo. The Bishop of Gozo (he said) had brought together the Gozitan parish priests to explain the significance of the Pastoral Letter on Integration. His Lordship had said that it was not "a political question" but a matter of the defence of the rights of the Church. "When asked what should be the conduct of confessors who are asked for their advice by penitents in confusion, His Lordship the Bishop had replied . . . that the Confessors should follow the principles they studied in Moral Theology. In the opinion of the authorities of the Church the new form of the Constitution without the required guarantees referring to the rights of the Church in Malta and Gozo cannot but be of great danger to our religion."[26]

On 9th February, Archbishop Gonzi spoke over the radio. No one listening to him could fail to understand what he was saying, nor remain ignorant of the deep rift between the Church and the Labour Party. The tone of the broadcast was sharp, the message clear. "It has been stated", said the Archbishop, "by word and in writing that in the Pastoral Letter of January 21 the Church gave no directives regarding the Referendum . . . But who reads that Document carefully and without prejudice must see that the Church gave a fundamental *directive* so that one can know how he

The 1956 Referendum

must behave . . ." Much of the broadcast was an attack on the Labour Government which "rose against the Bishops and broke relations with the Church without thinking twice. We were not surprised with this declaration of war (or with the) vulgar insults and mean insinuations against the Church's Authorities and the Clergy". Integration as proposed by the government was designed to secure economic benefits, but aid was likely to be forthcoming from Britain with or without integration, and the "political social and economic incorporation of small Catholic Malta with Protestant England could not but bring perils to the Faith and Morals of our People". The Church needed written guarantees and the Archbishop was prepared to fly to London to secure them. Then perhaps, with "appropriate and satisfactory" guarantees,

> We would have been able to tell you that from the religious aspect there is nothing to be said against Integration . . . As things stand at present, we cannot tell you this.

There was a last round of mutual recrimination before the voting. Mintoff broadcast a reply to the Archbishop, protesting that he had no wish to wage war on the Church—providing it kept out of politics; the Curia denied that there was any question of Labour Party supporters being excommunicated or refused absolution—all that the Church wanted were its "guarantees". As tempers mounted, there were excited scenes in a number of towns and villages. Speakers at a Constitutional Party rally at Tigne Wharf in Sliema were attacked by Labour Party supporters; scuffles broke out between members of Church congregations.

Local party groups quarrelled over court cases, as when Father Clement Caruana, a Carmelite prior, was acquitted on a charge that he had publicly defamed Mintoff. "There was a procession afterwards of people holding candles and applauding, carrying Father Caruana shoulder high up Old Bakery Street, singing Maltese and Papal hymns, to the Archiepiscopal Curia where Father Alwig said: 'The Church never errs. We thank God the Court has seen where the truth lies. Let us thank Our Lady.' The crowd sang Ave Maria. . . . Again Father Caruana was carried shoulder high to the Carmelite Church in Old Theatre Street where the people knelt down and the Church echoed to the glorious strains of the Te Deum. Fighting broke out later that evening." But the Church was not always triumphant. When part of the Archbishop's broadcast Statement on integration was read out in a number of churches, protests were made. "Some people left the church as soon as the speech was read, others shouted slogans and were then removed . . . Canon Saliba was reading the speech when two men left the church; the third, shouting 'Stop it', left the church too. Canon Saliba fainted, and was assisted to the sacristy."[27]

Throughout these verbal (and sometimes more than verbal) battles, Mintoff never wavered: he, the war and fortune's son, marched indefatigably on, and neither the Church nor the Nationalist opposition nor the Constitutionalist Party was able to stop the referendum. But one can now understand why the proportion of registered voters who either abstained or opposed was so large: nearly 80,000 out of 150,000.[28] Moreover, although Mintoff was resolute up to the point of the

Dom Mintoff in 1955.

Borg Olivier in 1956.

Archbishop Michael Gonzi (photographed in 1964).

Lord Strickland (1861–1940).

The 1956 Referendum

referendum it is possible to detect the beginning of uncertainty—of confidence turning to doubt—in the months which followed the voting.[29] It is no part of this brief account to tell the detailed story of the collapse of the integration proposals, but it would be absurd to leave the narrative at this high point of drama, the Labour Party seemingly having achieved its aim of making Malta part of the United Kingdom; the Nationalists, Constitutionalists, and the Church having apparently failed in their campaign to prevent it. Something needs to be said therefore about the way in which Mintoff began to draw back from his own proposals until he reached a point (exceeding that of his rivals) of direct opposition to his former ally, the British government.

The critical months were between February 1956 and April 1958. They began with the pretence of normality, it being argued by both governments that since a referendum had been held, and a favourable vote obtained, negotiations could begin to give the effect of law to the conference proposals. But there were undercurrents of tension. The results of the referendum had clearly fallen short of the enthusiasm for integration which the Round Table Conference had assumed would be demonstrated. The United Kingdom government professed itself willing still to go forward with the proposals: but—as will be seen—it added a further precondition: that there should be a general election in Malta before final approval for representation at Westminster should be given. Mintoff on the other hand—in explaining the measures which needed to be taken—now laid particular stress on the question of an interim financial agreement between the Maltese and British governments. Finance and integration (he said) went together, and help was needed not only to meet the current deficit on social services expenditure,[30] but to provide for capital expenditure during 1956 in order to strengthen the economy as a whole.[31] Certainly (said Mintoff) there were benefits to be drawn from the proposals. "Integration, which after all means no more than that two peoples have offered each other the hand of friendship to secure mutual assistance with due respect to all that each holds dear, has already created a new atmosphere which has rendered possible the progress of the Maltese people." But it was also "only an instrument, a great means by which we can stride forward . . . to a standard of life equal to that of the peoples who have ruled over us".[32] The Maltese delegation which had visited London to discuss these negotiations, had not been content with vague promises: it had insisted that the question of financial help should be given firm and clear guarantees, without equivocation, and the Labour Party would not yield on the issue. Indeed, if integration were now to fail, the Labour Party would insist on "immediate and full independence".

Thus the shadow of future quarrels began to fall across the bright hopes of the present, and by April 1958 all was ended: integration had been abandoned, the Labour Party was demanding separation from Britain, the Nationalist Party was refusing to cooperate, and once again—as in 1903, as in 1933—the constitution was suspended. Everything had gone

The 1956 Referendum

awry: for the Labour Party, for the Nationalists, and for the British Government.

This ruin of the Labour Party's hopes was self-imposed—according to H.M. Government in Britain: the charge brought by the Malta Labour Party and its allies was that the fault lay in London. The quarrel over aid, and the question of independence which led to the final break, are set out in an angry exchange of letters and memoranda, published in Valletta early in 1959, between Mr. Lennox Boyd and Mr. Mintoff.[33] Who was right? Who was in the wrong? On the evidence published by the United Kingdom and the Malta Labour Party the balance of argument in 1958-9 —when the constitution was suspended—might be thought to lie with the British Government. They, after all, were the more aggrieved. They had agreed to integration; they believed the proposals to be reasonable and generous; they were ready to implement all or part of them; they were convinced that the level of aid given to the Maltese islands compared very favourably indeed with that extended to other colonies.[34] They were even prepared to understand Mintoff's change of policy over integration but not his stated reasons for doing so, and they rejected indignantly Mintoff's charge that they were principally to blame.

A note of irritation as well as indignation runs through the correspondence. To the Colonial Office— no doubt to the British Government as a whole—Mintoff was a difficult, erratic, unstable leader who, because he was thwarted at home, behaved unreasonably abroad. If, said the Secretary of State, "the leaders and the Malta Workers' Union persist in their attitude of non co-operation, they must take their share of the blame for any failure of the enterprise and the consequences for Malta ". The consequences were likely to be unpleasant in view of the proposed transfer of the dockyards to Messrs. C. H. Bailey, since "although substantial assistance, financial and otherwise, is being given to this project by Her Majesty's Government, it is a commercial enterprise and will run the normal commercial risks accentuated by its dependence on attracting new trade to Malta". In such a context, quite apart from Commonwealth and N.A.T.O. interests, "we cannot in my view have profitable talks unless you recognise that the demand for 'immediate and full independence' is quite unrealistic. You are apparently unwilling to do this. . . . My view is based on the certainty that acceptance of your demand for 'immediate and full independence' would cause mass unemployment and untold suffering to the people of Malta. This is equally true for independence by January 1962".

That was in November-December 1958. And in February the following year the Secretary of State reviewed the melancholy sequence of events which had led to rioting in Valletta, the resignation of Mr. Mintoff, the refusal by Dr. Borg Olivier to form an alternative government, the November conference in London, further disturbances, and the suspension of the constitution. "After lengthy correspondence", Mr. Lennox Boyd reminded the House, "I persuaded Mr. Mintoff to come to London in March 1958. He asked then for further extensive financial commitments by H.M. Government or, alternatively, for the grant of

The 1956 Referendum

independence. . . . It was then clear that the prospects of integration were fast disappearing. In an effort to bridge the gap Her Majesty's Government offered an interim constitution for five years, broadly corresponding to full integration but without the provisions specially designed for constitutional integration of Malta with the United Kingdom. . . . Unhappily, however, it was not possible to make any progress with Mintoff on this basis." And the Secretary of State continued:

Indeed, soon after [Mr. Mintoff's] return to Malta, and without any clearance with Her Majesty's Government, he proposed a budget which would have involved a deficit of £7 million, all of which would have to have been met by Her Majesty's Government's alleged refusal to find a *modus vivendi* on financial aid for the period necessary to hold an election. He refused to form a caretaker Government, but agreed to remain in office while the Governor consulted the Opposition.
By this time, as the House will recall, there was serious rioting in Malta, which increased in violence over the next two days. Dr. Borg Olivier, the Leader of the Opposition, refused to form a caretaker Government. On 23rd April the Maltese Commissioner of Police told the Governor that Mr. Mintoff in his capacity as Minister of Police had issued orders, at three minutes' notice: one, to withdraw the mounted police; two, to suspend all baton charges; and three, to dismiss two named police officers. In the Commissioner's view—there were riots going on at that very moment—if these orders were carried out the Commissioner could not accept responsibility for keeping the situation under control. Therefore, in the interests of public safety, the Governor countermanded these orders and told Mr. Mintoff so as soon as he could contact him.
On the next day, 24th April, the Governor told Mr.

Mintoff that Her Majesty's Government were prepared to give financial assistance for the period of an election campaign at an annual rate of £5 million, without any conditions as to the situation after the formation of a new Government. At the same time, he asked for assurances from Mr. Mintoff that he would carry out his responsibilities for maintaining law and order. Mr. Mintoff was not prepared to give these, and the Governor, therefore, accepted his resignation. Then, as the House knows, there was a strike and a state of emergency was declared.[35]

The British Government were clearly exasperated, and the steps taken subsequently by Mintoff were adduced as further evidence of his waywardness. The Labour Party began to talk not only in terms of the right of self-determination but to draw parallels between Malta and Cyprus. A "Statement of Policy" issued by the National Executive in 1961 claimed that "had there been complete unity in Malta on this national problem, had the clergy been willing to co-operate with the Liberation Movement as in Cyprus, the pressure from the home front would have been sufficient to make the British Government recognise the Maltese People's right to self-determination. . . . In the prevailing circumstances it is not possible to put in the field a group of Maltese terrorists and carry out guerrilla warfare against the British occupation forces. It is for this reason that the Party adopted the policy of passive resistance". The Executive also began to look for new allies abroad, sending a delegation to Cairo in April 1960 and approving affiliation of the party with the Afro-Asian People's Solidarity Organisation—a bizarre gesture which was seized on by Mintoff's opponents as proof of the sinfulness of "any

The 1956 Referendum

support for the leaders of the Malta Labour Party so long as they remain at war with the Church and maintain contacts with Socialists, Communists, and the Afro-Asian People's Solidarity Organisation".[36]

By 1961, therefore, integration had not simply receded. It had disappeared totally beyond the horizon of what was either practical or desirable. But was it wholly Mintoff's fault? To some extent of course it was. He had tried to hurry the referendum through; he had misjudged the strength of the opposition to integration. He was as ready after 1956 to jettison the proposals as he had once been eager to formulate them. H.M. Government was thus able to lay the blame for the breakdown of the 1947 constitution at Mintoff's door and to explain the failure of integration to Mintoff's own, particular style of leadership—impatient of advice, extravagant in demands, even more extravagant of language, quick to change from protestations of affection to charges of deceit—a catalogue of sins which the British had been willing apparently to condone before, but not after, the proposals for integration had begun to be abandoned. Yet it would be wrong to place the blame wholly on one side. There were changes to in British policy which were of direct concern to the Malta Labour Government—as London itself was to acknowledge. The little pamphlet on Malta issued in May 1963 by the Central Office of Information noted that "a contributory reason to the failure of the integration talks was the fear entertained by the Maltese about the future of the dockyard and naval base, as these played a vital role in the Maltese economy". The Service Departments were still the largest single employers of labour "with an average of 19,416 employees out of a total labour force of about 83,000 between 1953 and 1957". And in February 1957, in the context of the integration proposals, "a remedial clause" was drawn up which provided that assistance would be given by Britain if, for six months, the level of unemployment in Malta remained higher than that in Britain owing to changes in imperial defence policy. Two months later, however, Mr. Duncan Sandys, then Minister for Defence, announced that "large reductions in manpower would inevitably curtail the volume of civilian employment in the naval dockyards and the ancillary establishments".

It is true that assurances were given again that the cuts would not begin to take major effect until 1960; but they were a dismal accompaniment to the negotiations over integration—how dismal may be seen from the troubled history of the dockyards under Messrs. C. E. Bailey Limited when the company took control of a substantial section of the Admiralty's dock labour force in 1958-9.[87] They help to explain not only why the Maltese Assembly unanimously passed a resolution (tabled by Mintoff in December, 1957) threatening the abrogation of all agreements with Britain, but the souring of the London talks the following year. Uncertainty over the level of British defence expenditure was always likely to lead to suspicion, particularly in the Malta Labour Party. And, against the background of uncertainty over the referendum results, Mintoff's change of heart and policy is more easily understandable. One can also see now, in retrospect, looking back over the muddled succession of Defence White Papers,

The 1956 Referendum

that the anxiety of the Malta Labour Party and the General Workers' Union about future changes in British defence policies—changes largely in the direction of a shrinking of British commitments overseas—was by no means groundless. Mintoff was perhaps more alert to these early signs of change than many of his contemporaries. And if the abrupt reversals of attitude on the part of the Malta Labour Party seemed incomprehensible—and irresponsible—at the time, they appear much less so today. It is the British side of the debate which has not worn at all well. By the beginning of the 1960's, for example, in the difficult and anxious debate over the United Kingdom economy and its indebtedness, defence expenditure was an easy target. A ceiling of £2,000 million was imposed in 1964, and the Labour Government began to move towards its decision to withdraw all British defence forces from "east of Suez" by 1971.[38] The "impossibility of full independence" had also been overcome not only for Malta but even smaller states, and for peoples very different from the Maltese—peoples almost without a national history. Indeed the United Kingdom has been foremost among the European colonial powers in reducing the requirements for independence in terms of the size, number, and poverty of resources of its former territories. It has rid itself of empire down almost to the smallest colony while protesting at every stage that it could and would not permit it. In 1956 it might have been thought that the Anglo-French attack on Suez, mounted partly from Malta, was evidence of a readiness by both countries to assert their interests throughout the world. But that was not so. Despite the conflict with Indonesia, despite repeated announcements by successive British Governments that they were determined to maintain a world role, withdrawal (it seems) was inescapable. Decolonisation proceeded apace—the Sudan in 1956, Ghana in 1957, almost the whole of British rule in Africa within the next decade.

Where then was the *raison d'être* for integration? The proposals put forward by Mintoff and accepted by the British Government rested on two major assumptions: that there existed a degree of common identity and a bond of common interests between the Maltese and British peoples sufficient to form a basis for union. The results of the referendum had cast doubt on the willingness of the Maltese to accept the argument of common identity; but between 1956 and 1964 the policy of the British Government, particularly over defence expenditure, began to cast doubt on the other principle of common interests. What those interests were could be argued about at length, as the Round Table Conference had tried to do, in terms of common values and shared beliefs about the nature of politics and the destiny of mankind: but they were also the reflection of a Commonwealth and Empire which was part of an established world order. Integration and Imperial defence were bound up together. They were two sides of a mutual bargain confirmed by the promise of economic aid and employment for the smaller partner. That was how Mintoff and the Labour Party had argued the case for integration: but if the Imperial side to these common interests were to be wound up, what point was there in pursuing the other half of the bargain?

PART III

Separation

> Who clipped the lion's wings
> And flea'd his rump and pared his claws?

Now at last we can turn to the very interesting question of what the British thought they were doing when they agreed to integration. At first one is baffled. Three Maltese in the House of Commons! Mr. Mintoff had succeeded where Joseph Chamberlain, Joseph Ward, and other early proponents of Imperial federation, had failed. The Maltese were to became part of the United Kingdom while retaining their own parliament in Valletta. In reaching such an agreement they had achieved a better bargain than many others had been able to secure; but, in essence, a process begun under the Tudors and extended under Anne and the Hanoverians was now apparently to be renewed: England, Wales, Scotland, Ireland, Ulster in 1921, and now Malta in 1956. Can one pick out some common thread of explanation from this long, slow expansion of Westminster? Perhaps it is to be found in a single word: defence—the defence first of England, then the United Kingdom, and finally of its "realms and territories overseas"? Because of its special position as an outlying defence post, Malta was to become part of the United Kingdom under a government still anxious to maintain its triple role of a Commonwealth, NATO, and world power? That surely is one explanation, or partial explanation, which may stand for the present.

But why integration? Why not a continuation, in suitably modified form, of the self-governing status which had been granted to Malta in 1947? Diarchy was no doubt difficult; but why should it be thought that integration was easy? If the mutual respect and goodwill which had been expressed so strongly by the Round Table Conference was sufficient to bring about integration, why should it not also be sufficient to sustain a sensible, working arrangement between London and Valletta in terms of their own mutual, defence interests? The spread of empire was very large: was there no room within it for a "self-governing Fortress Colony"?

There were no simple answers to questions of this kind except to say that the post-war world was not like that. It was not at all favourable to the continuance of colonial rule in its classic imperial form under any guise, however mild or generous or limited it might be. Already the greatest of empires had begun to dissolve into the modern world of sovereign, nationalist states: India, Pakistan, Ceylon. After 1947 the gates were wide open to the demands of other Asian—and African—leaders. And not only the British but the Dutch—and even the French—were busily engaged in unburdening themselves, quite prepared now to invoke the name of freedom "to cloak their weariness". In good time, too, no doubt; and certainly the writer has no wish to be misunderstood in terms of his own dislike of a great deal that was done—often innocently, sometimes malignantly—in the name of empire. Now at last the British have been freed of the need to rule others, and are surely the better for it; and some at least of those they ruled have been made to face the problems of power, and are the wiser for it. An awareness that the sun was setting finally over the whole range of empire was already widespread in 1956 among observers and practitioners alike. "The position of a dependency, ruled over by an alien Power", Professor Hawtry noted, "has come to be regarded as an anomaly not to be tolerated as a permanency".[1] So too Mr. Duncan Sandys who claimed not only to make a virtue but a profit out of necessity. Colonies, he thought, were a nuisance: "politically they involve us in much unwelcome controversy with the outside world; and economically we draw no profit from our sovereignty".[2] Very soon the greatest master of them all was to take Britain not only out of Africa but almost out of the Commonwealth in those uneasy years after Suez when perhaps only a Conservative Party under a radical conservative leader could have brought the British electorate to believe that the end of an old empire was the beginning of a new Europe.[3]

Where London led, Malta was not far behind. It was, after all, particularly galling to watch from Valletta—an ancient capital of a long established nation which was still a colony—the movement into independence of peoples who had been thrown together into the artifact of a colonial state by rulers whom they were now repudiating. So at least it seemed to a nationalist Maltese lawyer, Dr. Ragonesi. An ardent supporter of Dr. Borg Olivier, he was later to write an indignant letter to the *Times of Malta*[4] saying that: "The Maltese people yearn for self-government if only to put an end to the humiliation of being the only European people this side of the Iron Curtain to be denied home-rule . . .". Dr. Ragonesi was a little ahead of his time. But already the conviction was growing—not only in Valletta—that there had to be an end in one form or another to colonial rule wherever a suitable way forward could be found.

But there was still the apparently insuperable obstacle of Malta's fortress position. A curious aspect of the period of decolonisation was the continuation of a belief in both London and Paris that the loss of empire would not affect the Great Power standing of Britain and France. A country which had lost a world empire was still to play a world role—a belief sustained in Britain by the mystique of the Commonwealth and in France by the phenomenon of *Gaulisme*. No matter that Conservative Party leaders had earlier believed categorically that empire and power went together: that "if the British Empire were to break up, Britain would become a third class power".[5] The Empire had gone, but no matter: Britain was still the centre of a Commonwealth. The Commonwealth was an association of independent units, each of which was quite capable of acting against the interests of its fellow members. No matter; Britain was still a world power, with a world role to perform, and a world position to maintain. Churchill had said it. Eden believed it. Even Macmillan tried to believe it. Alas! And as late as

Separation

1964, almost a decade after the events recorded in the monograph, the Labour Party entered office under a leader who still clung to the belief: "I want to make it quite clear", said Mr. Wilson in his first speech as Prime Minister, "that whatever we do in the field of cost effectiveness, value for money and a stringent view of expenditure, we cannot afford to relinquish our world role . . ."[6]

Move back then to 1956, on the eve of the last joint venture by Britain and France, and one can understand why both the Round Table Conference and the Conservative Government under Sir Anthony Eden were unable to see Malta as an independent, sovereign state. The international scene was too dangerous and the situation in the Near East too disturbed for Britain to surrender control of the strategic centre of the Mediterranean: Malta was a NATO headquarters, adding an international dimension to the already complicated relationship between London and the Maltese Government. The islands for their part were too small; they had too few people; they were poor; they had little hope on their own of becoming rich. And, more particularly, they were unable to defend either themselves or the great naval base on which they depended for their livelihood. So independence had to be ruled out. The "political aspirations" of the Maltese were in "conflict with the requirements of her own defence and that of the free world".[7] And—one was able to add—it was as well for the Maltese that the island contained so magnificent a harbour and base to provide employment for its people.

Integration on the other hand seemed to resolve

many of these difficulties at a single bound. It put an end to the colonial status of the islands without thrusting them—small and helpless—into the sharklike world of sovereign states. It was even in accord with U.N. doctrine, in terms of the "free association [of a colonial territory] with the metropolitan or other country as an integral part of that country"—provided it was done "freely and on the basis of absolute equality".[8] It safeguarded Commonwealth and NATO interests while providing the Maltese with access to the wider democratic arena of British politics. It held out the promise of wealth and employment. And, by no means least in consideration, it gave expression to those mutual protestations of loyalty and affection which so impressed the members of the Round Table Conference. Reasons enough to pursue these "alternatives" to both empire and independence. Therefore we can say that integration was born at a particular point in time, at the confluence of two broad streams of British policy: the onward flow of decolonisation, which was later to carry the islands into full independence; and the continuing belief in London, which held Malta back from sovereignty, that Britain had still to undertake a lion's share of the defence and fortunes of the free world.

It is time now to pause and ask a question—at this very late stage—that can only be answered incompletely, namely: what sort of people are the Maltese, and what really was their relationship to Britain and the British? The fact is that they do not fall easily into any of the usual categories. They are "European" —yes: but almost certainly of Semitic origin. Many of

Mabel Strickland addressing a political meeting, the first to be held after the lifting of the ban imposed by the governor on public meetings after the resignation of Dom Mintoff's government.

Mabel Strickland and Paul Boffa.

A contested election, 1955. Malta's governing Labour Party attempting to break up an opposition Nationalist Party meeting called to protest against Labour's plan for the integration of Malta and Britain.

Separation

them speak English, but it is not their mother tongue as we know now from the history of the language controversy of the inter-war years. They do not "belong" to British history in the way that Australians and New Zealanders or (many) Canadians and South Africans can be said to derive their culture—including their political culture—from Britain. Indeed, the Maltese have a longer continuous history than the British; yet it was not until the early nineteenth century that the two peoples came in close contact with each other. In short, they are not at all like the inhabitants of, say, the Isle of Wight or the Isle of Man, or even the Channel Islands, or the Orkneys and Shetlands. They are Mediterranean people—"industrious, thrifty, courteous and law-abiding, still deeply religious, with strong family ties": quarrelsome, too, "with a vein of irresponsibility" (so Sir Hilary Blood thought) "financial and otherwise". Not always easy to govern, sweetness turning quickly to gall when offence is given; rough in politics, with a sharp tongue and easy wit, though tolerant too, and perhaps having to be so in their small islands whose honey-coloured fortifications look down on the open sea and its invaders. A close-knit community, notwithstanding the many illiterate and semi-literate,[9] and fortunate in having "at the other extreme . . . a proportion of highly educated, cultured people with a legitimate pride in their long history as a civilised and Christian people . . . well able to take their part as efficient members of a modern society".[10]

Their ties with Britain—certainly prior to 1956—were close enough to enable one to speak of a "special relationship". In what other context could one have had the remarkable career of Lord Strickland as a member of both parliaments—the House of Commns and the Maltese legislature? Strickland, of course, had thought of Anglo-Maltese in federal terms from a very early date at a time when such notions were fashionable, and had set out his beliefs in a letter to the London *Times* from Trinity College, Cambridge: "Sir, with a better form of Government and full political rights, the Maltese will soon be fitted to return a representation to the Imperial Federal Parliament on the same footing as Anglesey and the Shetlands. Thus only can the true British spirit be awakened and maintained among 150,000 European and British subjects . . . and thus can Malta become more really one with Great Britain."[11] Strickland, to be sure, was a fierce Imperialist, challenged fiercely by the Church and Mizzi's "Italian faction"; but there were many others who combined Maltese, British and Imperial careers very happily: Chev. Attilio Scebberas, for example, who at the turn of the century (like his brother before him) was a colonel in charge of a British regiment in India. At a humbler level, the Maltese had gratefully accepted its Imperial protector, and had really done very well under its rule not least through the encouragement deliberately given by the colonial government during the inter-war years to the language and civic rights of the majority of the people. True, there were riots in 1919 and 1931, true also that the constitutional history of the islands had been cut across by quarrels between Malta and Britain. But the strong attachment to British ways—and to the British themselves—persisted, as Commission after Commission, puzzled by what to do about the problems of joint control, were eager to record.[12]

On the Maltese side, therefore, affection went along with interest. And perhaps it is not too simple an assumption to believe that the welcome given by Britain to Mintoff's proposals included a substantial element of surprise and gratitude that there should still be a colony—in the post-war world of nationalist agitation—so old-fashioned as to wish actually to draw closer to the Imperial power:

> We are being asked to take a step [said Mr. Roy Jenkins in the Commons, speaking in the debate on integration] which is certainly novel in the history of the United Kingdom constitutional development, but it is no more novel than the spectacle which one saw in Malta six weeks ago of a meeting of perhaps 10,000 or even 15,000 people, mainly dockyard workers, waving Union Jacks, and crying "Long Live England". I think that in those circumstances we should be very foolish to be afraid of taking a novel but important step.[13]

The writer would add, too, his approval, not only in the light of a limited stay in the islands (during the early part of 1965), but in terms of the political history of Malta since 1964 when independence was at last attained. It has so far justified those who argued that the Maltese have taken firm hold of the political legacy of a parliamentary system translated from Westminster to Valletta. Debates in the lovely House of Assembly (the former Palace of the Knights) are in Maltese; they are often rowdy but the underlying form and conventions and the openness of debate in political life in and outside parliament—despite the enmity between the Church and many Labour Party supporters —place Malta among the few parliamentary democracies of the "third world".[14]

And the British? We turn back to the main theme of this last section. What was their attitude? The United Kingdom Government was conscious of the conflicting pulls of defence, which went against independence, and of the need to hasten Britain's withdrawal from empire. But what was the general drift of informed opinion in Britain in so far as it existed in any strength? One cannot be sure: but a great deal of back bench opinion in the House of Commons, and informed newspaper comment at the time, was not always favourable; sympathetic to the needs of the Maltese, yes, certainly, both before and after the 1956 referendum, but marked, too, by an uneasy alarm over the prospect of integration, particularly after the outcome of the voting was known. That was certainly true of the debate in the Commons on 26th March 1956 introduced by Lennox Boyd on the motion that this House "takes note of the Report of the Malta Round Table Conference 1955".[15] One must remember that the Conservative Government under Sir Anthony Eden was already trying to grapple with the much greater problem of Cyprus. Earlier that month, deportation orders had been served against Archbishop Makarios, the Bishop of Kyrenia, and two others; they were already on their way to the Seychelles, and violence—once again—had made British rule hazardous in this other Mediterranean island, some of whose leaders were also demanding "integration"— though not with Britain. There had been angry ex-

Separation

changes on that occasion in the House between Conservative, Labour and Liberal spokesmen. Now these differences were shelved in the calm, sensible, often intelligent, often very well informed, debate on Malta. The argument ran up and down the benches as much as across the chamber, and both affection and admiration for the George Cross Island were expressed. Yet there was an undertone of hesitancy, as if members were already beginning to doubt their own advocacy of the Round Table's Report, and there was opposition to as well as approval for integration.

In the interesting, muddled way that the House of Commons has of bringing into the debate virtually all the relevant data, speaker after speaker—including those who had signed and those who had dissented from the majority recommendations of the Report—circled round and round the main areas of controversy. Malta was a base, on which the people were absolutely dependent for employment; it was a Colony whose leaders had every right to ask for an end to their dependent status: a dilemma which could be met only by freely entering the democratic society of a sovereign state as Newfoundland had done in 1948 when it became the tenth province of Canada. Integration, therefore, was not only flattering to Britain: it made good sense for Malta—the only sense, as Aneurin Bevan tried to argue in a curiously Imperial anti-Imperialist speech:

When the proposal for integration was accepted by the people of Malta at its own election [in 1955] it was, for us, a very attractive proposition. It was much more congenial to hear of some Colony wishing to set up its home under

the paternal roof than to set up house on its own. . . .
[But] we were not prepared to accept the proposal and recommend it to Parliament merely because it marched so agreeably with whatever taint of imperialism might be left in some of us.
I am bound to say however that as our proceedings developed the logic of what has been called integration became quite inescapable.

The Nationalist Party's alternative, said Bevan, was so vague as to be undefinable. "I do not know what is quasi-Dominion status. . . . It seemed to us that Dr. Borg Olivier and his friends . . . accepting at the same time the dependence of Malta upon its fortress and therefore upon imperial finances, had not really worked out in detail their proposals in any way that we could understand. . . ." So the Round Table Conference was compelled "to consider the cogency" of the Maltese government's proposals for integration.

Other speakers reached the same conclusion. Malta, said Richard Crossman, was "economically as much a part of Britain as the population of Portsmouth, Devonport or Pembroke". Integration was simply the political complement to that economic fact. And since "our strategic necessities in the Mediterranean" required a base in Malta we ought "to secure the liberties of its people by binding them to us": otherwise "we shall lose the value of the base in Malta as we have lost the value of our base in Cyprus". Walter Elliot, the member for Glasgow, Kelvingrove, appealed to history—"not the history of a hundred and fifty years ago but of centuries ago: during that march of Asia and Africa to the West when the Knights were driven

Separation

out of Rhodes and established themselves in Malta. This morning we have seen Carthage voting herself into existence again—the new state of Tunis which, mark you, includes the great naval base of Bizerta. When Carthage is advancing, is that time to throw away one of our great watch-towers?"

It was not always easy to follow these flights of fancy. It was much simpler to concentrate on what the Maltese wanted: although that too was open to argument. "All who have studied this matter", observed Mr. Lennox Boyd, "agree that there can be no doubt that most Maltese do not like the present Constitution". But "how easy life would be—anyhow, in this matter—if they could agree on what they wanted!" There was the result of the referendum, in which "there was an affirmative answer by 75 per cent of those who voted, but the poll represented 44 per cent of those who were entitled to vote." What was one to make of that?

I would direct the attention of imperially minded Members of the House (said the Secretary of State) not only to the case of the Federation of Central Africa . . . but also to the referendum in Newfoundland where in the first referendum 88 per cent of the people voted, only 41 per cent of them voting in favour of confederation with Canada and, in the second referendum, 85 per cent voted of whom 54 per cent voted for confederation with Canada.[16]

No one liked the device of a referendum: it was un-English, "not a good expedient at all" said Aneurin Bevan. Lennox Boyd had also tried to dissuade Mintoff from holding it at too early a date, if only to avoid an open break with the Nationalists: but there it was.

And to opponents of integration it was plain that "whatever else may be said about the result what cannot be said is that it was clear and unmistakable".[17]

Mr. Vaughan-Morgan, member for Reigate, agreed. He had watched "the extraordinary referendum campaign" and he had "some doubts about the result". "We must take account of the fact that the majority of those who abstained were at least doubtful about, if not hostile to, these proposals." There ought therefore to be a further election in Malta to make sure that representation at Westminster was really wanted. Those, on the other hand, who approved of integration drew very different conclusions from the results. Speaking with all the authority of a former Colonial Secretary, James Griffiths agreed that a referendum was bad because of the danger of "irresponsible opposition": all one had to do was oppose without any fear of losing one's seat. But he went on:

> I regard the result . . . as a very big victory for the Malta Labour Government . . . in 1955 they fought the election on the same proposals . . . and polled 45 per cent. If the polling for the referendum had been polling for a general election the Malta Labour Party would have been returned with the same number of Members . . .
>
> What really caused the doubts about the referendum . . . was the fact that 40 per cent of the people abstained. It is anybody's guess how many of the abstainers were people who normally abstain . . . but in previous general elections the average abstention has been 23 per cent. If we assume that the number of ordinary abstainers . . . was the same as at a general election we can then say that the majority for the proposals was a very decisive one. Anyhow, there it is.

Separation

The argument was open to the charge that integration ought to have been a national not a party issue, although there was substance too in the general observation by John Foster, the Member for Northwich, that: "in referenda generally the abstentionist vote cannot be counted as an adverse vote. Admittedly, in [Malta] there is a special situation which allows a certain proportion of the abstentionists to be counted as opposing. Nevertheless, it is most remarkable that in a referendum 75 per cent of those voting said 'yes'."

So the debate went on, moving from point to point and back again. There was the problem, for example, of the rights and responsibilities of the three future Maltese members. They would have "equality of function with all the other Members, but not equality of responsibility"; they would be able to speak over the whole range of British affairs, but they would not be responsible to a constituency in the British isles, nor to a constituency in Malta for Maltese domestic affairs. It was also true (as Aneurin Bevan admitted) that the Maltese government would have "in its own field a far larger measure of power than is enjoyed by the Government of Northern Ireland. Of course, it will . . . [but] as Maltese members sit here and report back, and as we take a more lively and intimate interest in the affairs of Malta . . . it may be that we shall grow together"—an argument which the Catholic Church in Malta had every reason to distrust. The Ulster model was not a very happy example—the residual province of an unresolved civil war—yet it came as close as any to the constitution envisaged for Malta, adding one more anomaly to the constitution of the United King-

Malta and the End of Empire

dom itself, neither unitary nor federal but with working aspects of both in the way it functions: Ulster, the Isle of Man, the Scilly Isles, the Channel Islands, Lundy Island, and now Malta. The simplest hope, and much the least likely to be realised, was that expressed by Richard Crossman. " I should have liked [Malta] to become as close as an English county or an English county borough. I do not believe that integration will succeed, unless in the long run that happens; but we must be clear that it is not practical politics to propose it now." And it was on much the same uncertain basis of hope that most members were content to leave to the future the constitutional problem of Anglo/Maltese relations within the framework of the Report.

The question of Church and State was a much more sensitive area of debate since integration meant bringing a strongly Catholic island into a secular Protestant State. What would be the effect: and on whom? It was not a simple Catholic-Protestant dispute. Mr. Teeling, Member for Brighton, Pavilion, a Catholic, was against integration; Mr. Mellish, Member for Bermondsey—also a Catholic—was in favour. There were those who were apprehensive about the rights of the Church in Malta under the Protestant ascendancy of Britain, others who disliked the inclusion within the United Kingdom of a State in which questions of inheritance, marriage, bastardy, and a wide range of social customs, would be determined by Roman Law and Catholic practice. The Archbishop, said Teeling, was "terribly upset about what was to happen. He felt that in linking up with us, his country would be involved in various problems fundamental to themselves,

Separation

problems of education, of marriage, of birth control, and such things about which there is deep feeling in the island. He was terribly worried over the possibilities there. He wanted guarantees. He wanted signed guarantees, if possible. He felt that words were not good enough". Mr. Knox-Cunningham, Member for Antrim, South, was in full agreement about the danger of religious freedom: but on very different grounds. He was worried about the fate of Protestants in Malta. "Many years ago, the battle for Catholic emancipation in the United Kingdom was fought stoutly, and rightly won. The battle may again be joined but this time it will be for Protestant emancipation." Even Mr. Crossman's blood boiled at the misdeeds of the Church in Malta, and the Commons were presented with the rare spectacle of agreement between the Member for Coventry and the Member for Antrim South. "I am glad" (said Crossman) "that the hon. Member said what he did because there are certain things in Malta which really cause one's blood to boil. . . . I too come from the Protestant side [and] I must say that when I went to Malta I had to suppress a great deal of indignation inside me at what I saw there." Will it remain true, asked Mr. George Thomas, Member for Cardiff, West, that "when there are Members representing Malta in this House no Methodist minister will be allowed to wear his clerical collar in Malta, no Salvation Army officer will be allowed to wear his uniform, and there will be no freedom for Protestants?" Maybe, said Crossman, but "My reply to my hon. Friend is that we felt that the non-interference in the affairs of Malta must be both ways. If we do not interfere on the side of the Catholic Church we do not interfere on the side of the Protestants either." So again it was left to time to solve, with the belief (expressed once more by Crossman) that "in due course the people of Malta will do the right thing in their affairs".

A different part of the case for integration rested on the consequences (so it was argued) of not agreeing to Mintoff's proposals. Suppose one did nothing? Suppose one politely turned down the Malta Labour Party's suggestion and shelved the Round Table Report? Dire results had been prophesied by Mr. Teeling if integration went through.[18] What would happen if it did not? It was of course hard to say: but Mr. Roy Jenkins was not concerned about the Archbishop: Mintoff was the man with power.

The hon. Member for Brighton, Pavilion . . . said that we were building up a great deal too much on one party, perhaps even on one man, in Malta at the present time. I do not believe that anyone wants to do that in our relations with any one part of the Commonwealth. At the same time, it is difficult to visit Malta without getting the impression that the only leader of real force and ability is the present Prime Minister. It is difficult to build much on the other parties . . . or to believe that there is in Malta a situation in which there could be an alternative Government in the present circumstances.

Mr. Griffiths agreed. There was no answer to the Maltese problem but to say "We agree".

What alternative is there, because we must have an alternative? It is quite clear that, having turned down this proposal for integration, the present Government of Malta

Separation

would resign. They would seek a dissolution, there would be a general election, and what would it be about? I say frankly that that general election would be the beginning of a campaign for independence of some kind or other outside the Commonwealth, because we would then have blocked up all the roads to anything like political equality with the people of this country.

Such was the general feeling in the debate—that there was no alternative, and that the consequences of refusal were likely to be unpleasant. Cyprus was present in many members' minds. "We are anxious", said Bevan, "to see good relations between Malta and Great Britain; we are anxious to see that our interests there are properly served; we do not want to see on the Island of Malta a repetition of what has happened elsewhere"—a curious argument since not only was Archbishop Gonzi and the Roman Church in Malta much less militant than Archbishop Makarios and the Orthodox Church in Cyprus: the Church in Malta was directly opposed to the policy actually recommended by Bevan and the Round Table Conference. Indeed, there was a great deal more to be said (in this respect) for the argument advanced by Teeling than for that of his opponents: but the uneasy belief was very strong among members that since there was no way forward to full Dominion status the path to integration had to be taken.

What would be the wider consequences of adding Malta to the United Kingdom? We now reach the most interesting part of the debate. The House of Commons was quite content to alter other people's legislatures in the colonies—putting together or taking apart this or that federation—but it was extremely nervous about altering its own composition. Lennox Boyd in particular was careful to stress the "quite exceptional circumstances and position" of the island:

> There are, of course, and I know it well, a few other Colonial Territories in a similar position in so far as it does not appear likely that they can, under modern conditions, expect to achieve full self-government, including control of defence and external relations. But I genuinely believe that Malta is distinguished from these other territories in several ways. She joined the United Kingdom of her own free will. It is her own elected representatives who have asked for representation at Westminster. She is geographically close to the United Kingdom in distance and in time. She has a record of peculiar distinction and association with us in two world wars, and her economy and the lives of the greater number of her people are largely sustained by expenditure of Departments of the United Kingdom Government...
>
> Now, there are other territories to which one or more of these circumstances would apply, but to none do all of them apply in such a marked measure, and Her Majesty's Government feel able to endorse the argument in paragraph 77 of the Report that justification of Malta's claim to representation at Westminster can be based on the quite exceptional circumstances and position of the island.

It would be wrong (said Lennox Boyd) to suppose that no other territories would apply for representation: but each application could be considered on its merits and "so far as I can see such requests are most unlikely to be numerous".

The debate moved uneasily around the question raised by the Secretary of State. In a letter to *The*

Separation

Times that morning Miss Margery Perham had produced a list of twenty possible candidates.[19] How did members view that prospect? Some actually welcomed it in an outburst of enthusiasm for "imperial federation", some were very alarmed, most were uncomfortable. The range of emotion—emotion rather than reason—can be seen in extracts from the debate on this particular question:

Mr. Houghton (Sowerby): We do not believe that if this arrangement with Malta is reached it will be followed by other claims for representation at Westminster which could not be considered on their own merits. We believe that Malta is unique and that it has a claim to representation at Westminster on the basis of this constitutional solution. It is a claim far stronger than any other territory could have.

Mr. Teeling (Brighton, Pavilion): We begin to hear about Gibraltar and there is a suggestion about Cyprus. It is a possibility that in the long run someone may be able to find a solution whereby Cyprus could ask for representation. Then there are other areas, for instance the Seychelles. One cannot tell, but perhaps Archbishop Makarios might come to this House as a representative from the Seychelles —after having been there for a very long time—instead of as a representative from Cyprus. This matter may well become absurd . . .

Mr. Elliot (Glasgow): . . . Malta is a part of Europe. This is quite a different situation from that involved in the suggestion that we should integrate into our Parliament here far distant parts, separated in many ways much more widely from us than are the inhabitants of Malta. This case is *sui generis*, as the Conference decided, and this point of view could be defended on any platform to anybody.

Malta and the End of Empire

Mr. Crossman (Coventry): . . . it is quite unrealistic to deny the possibility that other countries—and here I am thinking of Gibraltar and the Gambia—if this arrangement works, will be inspired to dream of the same thing. It would be only sensible to view this as a precedent, which may be followed by other Colonies, if not by many.

Mr. Johnson (Rugby): . . . we could assimilate Malta—and, I suppose, the people of Gibraltar also—because they are part of Europe with a Latin culture, a Christian culture, and all the other things which go to make up our Western way of life. But what happens if the Gambia want to come in?

I was in Bathurst, Gambia, speaking to Mr. Garba Jahumpa and other leaders there, and they said, without any hesitation whatever, "If Malta comes into the United Kingdom Parliament, we, too, would like to be Members at Westminster." This might also apply, although I would not care to commit them, to Sierra Leone, or even Mauritius . . . if we do not take in Gambia, we are up against the question whether to admit only white and Europeans to this Parliament, or go beyond that stage and admit others of different colours.

I submit that once we begin by having Members for Malta in the House of Commons we shall have to go on to the Gambia and beyond, because we cannot stop at whites and Europeans only . . . if the smaller people, who look to us for guidance and regard us as a shield, decide to opt into this place and to pay us this compliment I say that we should allow them to come in.

Mr. Pitman (Bath): Clearly, the organisation and the real integration which ought to take place for Malta is the integration of a Commonwealth Government and a Commonwealth Parliament . . . It could flower into a great idea. It could apply potentially not only to the United Kingdom, the Dominions, and all the Colonies . . . Our friends from

Separation

Northern Ireland might easily find themselves in a much better position with their friends the other side of the border, and Ireland might easily come back into a Commonwealth organised on those lines.

Mr. Pickthorn (Carlton): The right hon. Member spoke about the thin end of the wedge argument. I saw, in a letter to *The Times* today, that someone had suggested that there might be as many as twenty applicants. I do not know how that may be. It is possible to argue that the thin end of the wedge argument is the best reason for integration, if we want Parliament to expand that way; but we ought to stop and think very deeply about that chance before we go any further.

Such a fuss! What would happen, it was asked, if the three Maltese M.P.s held the balance between Labour and Conservative? There was a difference of only 6 in 1950-51. Suppose it narrowed again in the future?[20] The Irish had been a problem in the last century: was Parliament to be disturbed again by new arrivals from Malta? Even those who were most welcoming tended to rest their case on necessity: there was no other way forward. And if the reader will bear patiently further quotations from the debate, the truth of the matter will out. There were two passages—one from a speech by Commander Agnew, Member for Worcestershire, South, the other by Richard Crossman —which (to the writer) seem to illustrate a central position held, under many guises, by speakers on both sides of the House. Commander Agnew was very blunt:

Although I personally regret that the situation should be such that we have to infiltrate Members from another country, Colony or Dependency into our Parliament to help us manage our domestic affairs, if that is to be the price in order to maintain in a firm and new unity the loyalty of this ancient Dependency with which we are so closely linked, and which has performed such great service for our kingdom, it is not too high a price to pay, and a scheme of union should go forward.

Crossman said much the same though less plainly: "It is perfectly fair for any hon. Member to say that he would like to look at this proposal very carefully indeed before accepting it, and to ask whether we are justified in doing it. It would say to the right hon. Member for Renfrew, West that if I saw any alternative way of holding Malta loyal, I would not myself have accepted this unprecedented action." The members of the Round Table Conference, said Crossman, "would not have been entitled to advise this House to accept integration unless we had seen it as the only possible way of dealing with the problem satisfactorily. I believe that it is only under those conditions that we are entitled to set this precedent".

Crossman's words were directed in particular to John Mackay (Renfrew, West), one of the two signatories of the Minority Report, whose main contribution to the debate had been to urge the need for caution: H.M. Government, he said, ought not to act precipitately but wait upon further events in Malta before granting representation at Westminster. And in the closing speech for the Labour Opposition, Griffiths came near to saying something very similar. He was still willing to stand by the substance of the Report, but now advocated action in two parts. The Government should

Separation

go ahead with all the necessary and attendant measures for integration; but that part of the Bill providing for representation in the House of Commons should wait not only upon the next election in Britain but on the outcome of a further election in Malta. "When that Bill has been carried through the House leaving the date upon which representation at Westminster becomes operative to be fixed by Order in Council, at that stage—Parliament having committed itself in a Bill—let us ask the people in Malta. Let us have a general election in Malta, and let the general election there either confirm or reject it. That, I think, is the way now in which we can proceed."[21]

Faced with this definite suggestion, Lennox Boyd backed away. He was very clear in his refusal. "I certainly did not say that there should be a third test in Malta. Malta has had a general election and a referendum. I did not say that another test would be essential before Her Majesty's Government took possible steps to give effect to our acceptance of the Report." Nor could he see any virtue in delay or in any alternative suggestion that had been made during the debate. Such was the conclusion reached by the Secretary of State in his closing speech, and the House was asked formally "to take note of the Report of the Malta Round Table Conference". Very plain, one might have thought, very precise, the way ahead cleared for action. But, alas, one can never be quite sure what a Secretary of State is actually trying to say. Three days later, the Prime Minister made a statement in the House which was very different in tone and substance. It is worth quoting in full:

As my right hon. Friend the Colonial Secretary told the House in Monday's debate, the Government accept the Report of the Round Table Conference and intend to proceed with the necessary steps to carry out its recommendations.

The Government have now considered, in the light of the debate, what these steps should be. They have decided to proceed with legislation in this House to give effect to the recommendations of the Report. The Bill will provide for all the necessary changes involved in carrying the Report into effect.

However, that part of the Bill relating to the representation of Malta in this House will be brought into operation only if and when the Maltese people have shown their desire for it in a General Election following a dissolution of the Maltese Legislative Assembly. The Prime Minister of Malta has said he will request the Governor to grant this.

The cabinet had had second thoughts, as Eden made clear in the first volume of his memoirs. Between the holding of the referendum and the debate in the House of Commons, a change of attitude had taken place: more cautious, less approving, more suspicious. The quarrels in Malta, wrote Eden, "had their consequences at home, where a number of Government supporters in Parliament showed increasing reluctance to accept Maltese representation at Westminster". The Prime Minister resisted "suggestions that the Report . . . be delayed" but "added one condition": that there should be a further election in Malta.[22]

The debate in Parliament ran parallel to similar arguments in the press. The correspondence columns in *The Times* took up the question: Borg Olivier versus Thomas Balogh, Margery Perham versus Edward Ellul; Mabel Strickland, Borg Olivier again, Protestant Anglicans, Roman Catholics, for and against integration, for and against Mintoff and his rivals. A month before the Commons debate, for example, Thomas Balogh—then economic adviser to the Malta Government—tried to uphold the Malta Labour Party by attacking its opponents. The Nationalist Party, he said in a letter to *The Times* on 23rd January, had "decided to boycott not because of the alleged abuses but because it has lost popular support on account of the complete bankruptcy of the negative policies of the former Government striving after prestige only. It hopes now that its case for abstention (to camouflage its failure) will be supported by the Roman Catholic Church . . . an attempt at abusing honourable religious scruples for religious purposes". A fortnight later, on 4th February, Borg Olivier replied—defending his party, and accusing the Maltese Government of trying to impose integration on a bewildered, ill-informed electorate: "75 per cent of the people over 35 are illiterate" and "are kept informed . . . through broadcasts which are literally monopolised by the Government". Then came the results of the referendum, and Borg Olivier sent a second letter, claiming that the electorate had actually given its decision very clearly, and that "one would have thought that the whole question should now be regarded at an end".

In its editorial on 15th February *The Times* foreshadowed the policy later adopted by Sir Anthony Eden. "The results of the Maltese referendum do not justify the introduction of the integration scheme with representation for the island at Westminster. A radical constitutional change of this kind requires, in common sense if not in law, a two-thirds majority." Mintoff had failed; and "as a spokesman of the Archbishop of Malta rightly said", the result "is not a clear and unmistakable expression of the wishes of the people". It was a pity. "A chance in history has been missed," but the fault lay with the Church and its resistance to "the winds of a modern secular, non-believing world" which were beginning to blow across the Maltese islands. The editorial looked kindly on Mintoff: he "had given the island the best local administration it has seen for years. Nobody understands the essence of the Maltese problem better than he does" . . . although he was also "impatient and sometimes creates incidents which gratuitously antagonise the hierarchy". Now there was nothing that anyone could do. The United Kingdom Government should accept that part of the Round Table Report which stressed the need to strengthen the machinery of consultation between London and Valletta, and be generous in its provison of aid: but it should abandon the notion of representation at Westminster. Mintoff might possibly "revive the idea of integration at a later date" if (*The Times* concluded) "opinion in Britain has not by then moved against it": a fair and prescient warning.

On the morning of the debate in the House of Commons, Margery Perham's letter to *The Times* was printed. It echoed earlier doubts about the wisdom— "in face of the most adverse historical lessons"—of opening Parliament to Maltese members. Precedents would be established which could not then be brushed aside. "There are 20 small territories, a majority of which, if not more, may one by one join the queue. Since young nationalists naturally have the emotional sense of prestige attached to the prima donna, it would be difficult to find any arguments acceptable to them which put them in a category different from that of Malta. . ." We should not, therefore, in our "too-British way drift today into a decision which may tie our hands in dealing with dependents which are literally world wide and whose small areas . . . are no measure of the size of their potential political difficulties".

In a final editorial on 26th March, *The Times* gave its support to those who were worried by the effect that integration would have on British politics. The three Maltese members (it argued) might "balance the vote in the House of Commons when the parties were evenly matched". And "with their different interests and background they might prove themselves a fractious element which would embarrass Parliament", particularly since there was "an even chance that the Maltese might send to Westminster, or elect in Malta itself, representatives who would frankly set out to boycott or sabotage integration". The proposals were also a dangerous precedent; they were a radical break with "traditional colonial policy", and borrowed too much from "the French system which is at the moment demonstrably breaking down in almost every part of the French empire". It was probably right therefore to abandon the scheme, particularly since "the clear sign needed for action had not been given" by the Maltese themselves.

If *The Times* was doubtful, opinion "more to the right" was openly hostile. "Even had the islanders declared themselves plainly and overwhelmingly in favour of integration", said the *Telegraph,* "there would remain serious doubt from the United Kingdom standpoint about the wisdom of a measure implying a fundamental change in the conception of our Parliament. To attempt such a legislation when the issue still sharply divided the Maltese themselves would be dangerous as well as unwise."[23] Even those of a less conservative persuasion were hesitant: the *Guardian* thought Mintoff should resign, the *News Chronicle* suggested another referendum, the *Herald* another election. Church newspapers entered the controversy, divided between a Catholic and Protestant conviction; but both were opposed to integration, either on the grounds that it would injure Catholics because of the hostility of the Malta Labour Party to the Church, or because of the undue power of the Church in Malta.[24]

To the sound of that chorus of dissent, integration faded and was forgotten. And already by the autumn of 1956 Malta and its problems were brushed aside by the passionate debate in Britain over the Anglo-French attack on Suez. Thereafter a great deal was changed, not least by the arrival in office of the first British Prime Minister who was prepared to weigh the new Commonwealth (and what remained of the old Empire) in the balance of national interest and find it wanting. From Suez to Brussels the road was short (though unrewarding) and by the end of the first negotiations to join the European Economic Community the imperial role of the United Kingdom had shrunk to a

Separation

very small measure. Indeed it must be very difficult today for anyone born, say, immediately after the war, or even in 1939, to believe in the recent existence of a British-ruled Empire which covered so large a part of the world. And in the rapid end to colonial rule between 1956 and 1964 Malta was simply one more island—one more colony—to be given a final constitution, a handsome gift or loan, membership of the Commonwealth, and a ceremonial farewell.

There were of course numerous petitions, meetings, delegations, discussions, conferences between the Maltese leaders, the Governor,[25] and the Secretary of State[26] after the reintroduction of Governor's rule in 1959. The details of these final stages before independence have been described very thoroughly by Professor Edith Dobie,[27] and there is no point in recounting them here. What needs to be noted, however, is the speed with which the islands moved towards independence. During the last years of colonial government Mintoff rode high on a great wave of indignation with Britain, cabling his protests to the President of the United States and the Secretary General of the United Nations, visiting Kruschev in Moscow, Nasser in Cairo, uttering warnings, and adopting brave postures of defiance rather like the Young Columbian:

Bring forth that Lion! Alone I dare him! I taunt that Lion! I tell that Lion, that Freedom's hand once twisted in his mane, he rolls a corse before me . . .

But really the poor Imperial lion was already moribund. And suddenly there was a reversal of the parts played by the chief actors in the drama. The Nationalists continued to ally themselves with the Church but now collaborated with the British; they accepted office after a further election in 1962 under a new constitution, and then sought approval to hold a referendum on a draft constitution for independence. Far from hesitating, the United Kingdom Government agreed not only to the referendum but to the grant of independence on the very slender basis of a bare majority for the Nationalists' proposals. Mintoff, on the other hand, having lost the election, instructed his followers to vote "No" in the referendum. The "centre parties"—the Democratic Nationalist Party, the Christian Workers Party, and Miss Strickland's Progressive Constitutionalists—were divided between opposition and boycott, but joined the M.L.P. in condemning Borg Olivier.

The critical turning points, therefore, were the two contests of 1962 and 1964 both held under the constitutional arrangements introduced after the *Report of the Malta Constitutional Commission*[28] had been presented to Parliament in February 1961. The constitution was a carefully drafted document which, seeking "a basis for partnership between two nations one large and one small, each of which still has need of the other", abandoned the concept of diarchy, and recommended the use of "concurrent powers". In practice, it was no more than an interim arrangement between the breakdown of the 1947 constitution and the early movement into independence, but it helped to ease the transition by enabling the February 1962 election to take place—an election fought bitterly throughout Malta and Gozo and involving almost the whole of the adult population: there was a 91 per cent poll. The General Workers Union gave close support to the Labour Party; the Church triumphant rode into battle alongside the nationalists and—as in 1932 so in 1962—the organised hostility of the Curia and its priests was decisive. Every device was adopted—Pastoral Letters, pamphlets, articles in *Lehen-is-Sewwa*,[29] nightly vigils, pilgrimages including the carrying in procession of Malta's holiest relic, the arm of St. Paul, the ringing of church bells to drown Labour Party speakers at local rallies, the use of Catholic Action, and the interdiction of the entire Labour Party executive—in a very successful attempt to offset the efficient network of Labour Party branches. Mintoff countered with attacks on the Church and on Borg Olivier. "The priests know that sooner or later the wind of change will also reach Malta's shores. . . . Will they succeed in throwing up in time a little Salazar who will keep tiny Malta tightly tied to their medieval conception of Christianity and private property?"[30] But the outcome was a defeat for the Labour Party:

	Seats
Nationalist Party	25
Malta Labour Party	16
Christian Worker Party*	4
Democratic National	4
Progressive Const.	1

*founded in 1961 by Anthony Pelligrini, former general secretary of the MLP, allegedly in an attempt to reconcile Labour Party supporters and the Church.

Borg Olivier became Prime Minister of the new

"State of Malta"—the title proposed by the Blood Commission[31]—and almost immediately opened negotiations with Duncan Sandys, now Secretary of State for the Colonies, for a final constitution and the grant of independence. "We in Britain", said Sandys, opening a Conference of Maltese delegations in London in July 1963, "have no desire to hustle Malta into independence or to lay down our responsibilities so long as you need us." Perhaps not. But there was no attempt now to describe "the unrealities of immediate and full independence". It was in the autumn of 1958, less than five years earlier, that Lennox Boyd had talked of "the certainty" that "independence would cause mass unemployment and untold suffering to the people of Malta". It was a different story in 1963, and on 1st August at the end of the conference (from which all but the Nationalist delegation had withdrawn) H.M. Government—in an attempt to force agreement between the Maltese leaders—actually appointed a day, 31st May, 1964, by which Malta should be independent. One can judge too how very different the British attitude had become by noting (in the following paragraphs) the readiness with which the Government accepted the outcome of the referendum—the last electoral contest endured by the Maltese prior to independence.

In 1956 the United Kingdom Government had been very sceptical of such devices. They now agreed to Borg Olivier's wording of a referendum which read: "Do you approve of the constitution approved by the Government of Malta, endorsed by the Legislative Assembly, and published in the Gazette?" The details

Separation

of the constitution had been presented by Borg Olivier to the London Conference, whereupon the Labour Party delegation had withdrawn in protest; submitted to the Malta Parliament, the constitution had been carried by 26 votes to 16. Mintoff had attacked the draft —and objected to the referendum—not because he was against independence but because it gave expression to the privileged position of the Church, and indeed the proposed draft constitution contained two clauses unique surely in modern times. "Nothing done by the Roman Catholic Church in the exercise of its spiritual powers or duties shall be held to be in contravention of any provision of this chapter [on Fundamental Rights and Freedom of the Individual]"; and "Nothing contained in or done under the authority of any law for the protection of the Religion of Malta shall be held to be inconsistent with or in contravention of any of the provisions of this chapter."[32] The Labour Party not only rejected these clauses, but wanted specific guarantees for the civil liberties of those who opposed the church hierarchy, and Mintoff proposed six amendments to the constitution: civil marriage should be permitted, the Church should not take part in politics, the Archbishop should not be exempt from the ordinary jurisdiction of the criminal courts, there should be no inflicting of spiritual injuries to influence voters, there should be freedom of belief for non-Catholics, and—though Roman Catholicism should be the state religion—parents should have the right to opt out of religious instruction for their children. None of the amendments at this stage of the negotiations was accepted, and the Archbishop announced that he would go to prison first, along with thousands of his followers, if there were any amendment to the Corrupt Practices Act to forbid the imposition of "spiritual religious penalties" on electors.

Here was the reverse of the situation in 1956 when the Church wanted written constitutional guarantees against the abuse of power by the Labour Government. But once again a referendum was held, this time under Nationalist Party auspices, and again the margin of difference between the two sides was close:

1. Registered Electors   162,743[83]
2. Voters   129,649 = 74%
3. For the Constitution   65,714 = 51.5% of (2); 40.3% of (1)
4. Against Constitution   54,919 = 43% of (2) ⎫
5. Blank or Spoiled   9,016 =   ⎬ 97,029 = 59.7% of (1)
6. Non-Voters   33,094 =   ⎭

Once more it could be argued that less than half the electorate had voted for the referendum, that is, for independence under the proposed constitution. Only 65,714 = 52 per cent (or, at best, 54.5 per cent if the number of spoiled or blank votes were eliminated) had voted in favour—a smaller number than those who had actually voted for integration in 1956. Nearly 60 per cent had voted against the proposal or had shown their disapproval by abstention or the spoiling of their ballot.

As in 1956, so in 1964, there was a post-referendum debate in the House of Commons, the prime purpose being to give parliamentary approval on one day— 23rd July, 1964—to the second reading, committee

Separation

stage and third reading of the Malta Independence Bill. It was among the last acts of the dying Parliament of the Conservative Government in its closing months in office. And Mr. Duncan Sandys would have it so. Too many discussions had taken place already for there to be any further merit in delay. The Maltese leaders had been unable to reach agreement among themselves, the "target date" for independence had come and gone, and it was time now to settle matters by an imposed compromise: amending the condition proposed by the Nationalist Government in order to meet some of the objections of the Malta Labour Party opposition. Such was the gist of the argument by the Secretary of State to an uneasy House of Commons. The referendum, said Sandys, should be ignored:

As it turned out, the referendum added nothing to what we already know about the division of opinion in Malta. Moreover the results were somewhat confused by the fact that the smaller parties which on the whole favoured the Constitution . . . did not feel able to vote for it lest their votes should be interpreted as implying approval for independence . . . After careful consideration I formed the opinion that the results of the referendum were not sufficiently conclusive to justify basing important decisions on them.[34]

It was by such arguments that independence was urged forward, the amendments to Borg Olivier's draft constitution being as follows. First, the insertion of a clause prohibiting discrimination on racial or religious grounds. Secondly, the deletion of Sections 48(10) and 48(11) of the Malta Government draft "which would have had the effect of exempting the Roman Catholic Church altogether from the application of the code of human rights". Other bargains were struck. There were the two Agreements on Finance and Defence—inseparable companions of every argument between Britain and Malta throughout the long history of their relationship. The Defence Agreement—said the Secretary of State—"enables British forces to remain in Malta for a period of 10 years after independence, and accords to them, by and large, the same military facilities which they enjoy at present". The Financial Agreement was tied to that on defence, and fell into two parts. There was the immediate provision of £600,000 budgetary aid for the current year, and the offer of £50 million for the next ten years, conditional after 1967 on the maintenance of the agreement on defence.

The debate which followed was uneasy, often resentful, in tone. Mintoff and his colleagues were still in London, lobbying the Government and the opposition, and members on both sides of the House pointed out that it was the first time—or almost the first time—that a colony had been given independence without a formal agreement on the constitution between local political leaders: Zanzibar was an exception, but that had led to revolution and murder. Where was the need for hurry? Why not wait and seek a further measure of agreement between the Maltese parties? The opposition, said Mr. Bottomley, would put down an amendment to provide "for elections to take place in Malta before independence", and he wanted to "make it clear that we on this side of the House say that the Govern-

Separation

ment themselves have the full responsibility for the content of the constitution". Mr. Griffiths added his own warning: "This constitution is not an agreed constitution, agreed between the Government of Britain and people representing the majority of those in Malta. . . . If the House of Commons agrees with the Bill we shall be adopting a constitution which has not been approved by the majority of the people in Malta."

Harsher words were used by other opposition speakers. The amendments proposed by the Government were said to be "worthless" since Clause 2 subsection 2 of the constitution was there still, namely: "The State guarantees to the Roman Catholic Apostolic Church the right freely to exercise her proper spiritual and ecclesiastical functions and duties and to manage her own affairs." On this basis, said Mr. Driberg (Member for Barking) the Constitution "may well result in—I will not say the establishment of, because there already is one, but the consolidation of a clerical dictatorship in Malta", blessed by the Vatican, and operated by "Archbishop Gonzi, and his puppet Prime Minister". Many Catholics in England, it was said, were critical of "the antique and unique Roman Catholic Establishment in Malta."[35] Why then should the House condone the abuses of the 1962 election, and why should it ignore the results of the April referendum?

But Mr. Sandys would have none of this kind of argument. The need was to get the deed done. Catholics and the Catholic Church had a special position in Malta just as Moslems and Islam had a special place in the constitution for Malaya. And "if we fail to pass

Malta and the End of Empire

the Bill now, it would be difficult to get independence much before the beginning of next year". Malta was not like Zanzibar or Guyana, said Mr. Sandys, the difference being that "while these people [in Malta] say rather beastly things about each other they do not kill or burn one another every night". Later in the day, Mr. Bottomley's amendment was moved in the Committee stage, when fresh arguments broke out again; it was defeated, and there was a final grudging acceptance by the whole House of the closing statement by the Secretary of State: "I really think that we have got to the point where we have to take it that we have decided that Malta is to be independent."[36] The Bill then went through its third reading among a dwindling number of members from both sides of the Commons, was passed by the Lords on 29th July,[37] and received the Royal Assent two days later.

Malta became independent at midnight on 20th–21st September, 1964, an object of contention to the last, both in Britain and Malta. Of course there were celebrations. Malta was now to be governed at last, and really for the first time in the long history of the Islands, by the Maltese themselves. The final ceremony was performed by H.R.H. The Duke of Edinburgh:

And now, Mr. Prime-Minister, it falls to me to perform the concluding act of British Sovereignty in these Islands, as I present to you these Constitutional Instruments which establish Malta's Independence. Long may it endure.

There was great jubilation therefore in Malta, Gozo, and Comino among thousands of Maltese, and from every quarter of Christendom emissaries arrived, bearing messages of goodwill: saints and fireworks, Church and State, Rome and London, Pope and Queen—all rejoicing together: though not Mr. Mintoff and his Labour Party executive.

So we reach the end of the story: not integration but independence. What can be said about the proposals by way of conclusion? Like a tiny mirror the story told in this essay reflects much larger themes, and it is time perhaps in these closing pages to end fact and try, not fiction, but conjecture.

Should we, for example, be sorry that Mintoff failed to carry his proposals? A little perhaps, since the relationship between Malta and Britain was founded on a genuine affection, and it is always sad to see affection dissipated. Yet it is also not difficult to reach the conclusion, looking back from the vantage point of a decade later in time, that it was well the story ended as it did. Integration (one can argue) would very likely have soured, not improved, relations between the two countries. It would have been at best an anomaly, once the full flight from empire had been achieved, at worst a disaster, ending in conflict as in Ireland and Ulster. Certainly the proposals left full scope for argument over what was meant by integration, and there would always have been the danger that disputes in Malta itself would have been carried to Westminster. Would Mintoff, for example, as a member of the House of Commons, have refrained from trying to enlist H.M. Government in London against the Church in Valletta, as Strickland had tried to do from the House of Lords in the 1930s? And had such issues been forced on a reluctant House of Commons would any Government in Britain in the 1960s have responded willingly to the need to settle such quarrels in a distant island province?

It was with these forebodings in mind perhaps, and because of the collapse of the negotiations in 1958, that neither the Conservative nor Labour Government repeated the offer of overseas representation at Westminster. Other islands or "smaller territories" were to be offered association not integration, an offer which preserved the separate identity of the particular colony, and kept its problems at a safe distance from Westminster. There was also a clear rejection by the United Kingdom Government of the programme of the "Integration with Britain Party" when it took office in Gibraltar under Major Peliza in the summer of 1969: a last fading echo of imperial federation from the one remaining colony in Europe. A near anomaly with Malta (one may judge) had been enough, quite apart from difficulties in Madrid.

Other themes can be picked out of the story. It was noted earlier, for example, that the transfer of power to the small fortress colony of Malta was strong evidence of the change in British fortunes during the post-war years. Indeed, in the brief period between the agreement on integration, and the actual grant of independence to Borg Olivier's Government, the retreat from empire was precipitate. Colonies were "pitchforked into independence overnight"[38] without local resources, without preparation, even without agreement (as in Malta) on the need for independence. And in time, the giving up of empire was matched by a similar withdrawal from the world at large; most noticeably

Separation

by the Labour Government in its decision not to remain "east of Suez"—that vast region of empires where future historians, musing amidst the ruins of Delhi or listening to the choirs of Buddhist monks, must surely look for an explanation of the rise and fall of British rule. So much is commonplace. But there is an interesting side to the integration proposals which has not yet been examined: not why they were formulated, nor why they were abandoned, but why they were received with such caution in London. It was almost as if both sides in the affair, Malta and Britain alike, accepted the recommendations of the Round Table conference despite themselves, knowing that—in essence—the British Commonwealth and Empire was not like that. The French Empire perhaps, but not the British, a distinction drawn in self-approving terms by several Members of the House of Commons during the 1956 debate. Why was there that reservation? What kind of imperialists were the British, to look so doubtfully at those who wished to draw closer to them? It is here in particular that conjecture, not argument, is needed.

Consider, for example, the view that would have been taken of similar proposals in Paris. We know what the answer would have been. No surprise or uncertainty there at suggestions of integration. In 1955 there were over eighty deputies in the French National Assembly from Algeria, and from the *départements* or *territoires d'outre-mer*. Réunion, Martinique, Guadeloupe—islands roughly comparable in size and population with Malta[39]—have been represented in Paris as overseas Departments since 1946: their representatives

Malta and the End of Empire

were still there in 1970. We know of course that in the end the French failed to match their practice with their principles. They were not prepared to run the risk that France might become "a colony of its colonies" by an extension of an equitable franchise to their overseas territories, and they too backed away from integration, finding a peaceful surrogate perhaps for empire—butter not guns?—in Brussels. Yet at its noblest, the French empire sought to emulate Rome in its vision of a single *respublica* and a common citizenship. Not so the British. Although very willing to export their institutions to those created in their image, they did so only on the basis of separate national units. "The object of colonisation", it was once said, "is the creation of so many happy Englands."[40] And it was to be done, not by incorporating the overseas colonies into a Greater Britain, but by the free association of "new nations"—first among Englishmen settled abroad, then by giving expression to "a sense of national consciousness"[41] among Asians, Africans, and an astonishing variety of peoples. If there was a model it was Greece, not Rome,[42] though in fact there has been no parallel in history to this deliberate attempt to transfer institutions and procedures shaped in the metropolitan country to virtually every territory brought under its rule.

No wonder, therefore, that the Maltese proposals were treated with such reserve. The wonder is that they were considered so seriously. Others had already tried and failed to move H.M. Government in the same direction—towards the concept of Imperial federation. Yet here was a further attempt to bring about a reversal

Separation

of the classic formula whereby colonies were transformed into self-governing nation states. Canada, New Zealand, Australia, white South Africa, India, Pakistan, Ceylon, Ghana—an imposing line of ex-colonies, from the very large to the very small, India and Malta alike, moving into the future, each sovereign and free, each patterned on Britain, although "home-made" in terms of the structure of its domestic politics. Such was the Durham formula by which a Commonwealth of Nations was brought into existence, reconciling empire and liberty. And against this onward sweep of history, it is easy to understand why, by 1964, the pull of independence in Malta was too strong, the doubts about integration in London too great, to be resisted.

The writer is not at all critical of the Durham formula, however doubtful he may be about the speed with which the transfer of power was finally carried through. Over a wide range of colonial problems it can be argued that the British were more perceptive and, *mirabile dictu,* more logical than the French in the sense that, stumbling from precedent to precedent, they came to terms at a very early date with colonial nationalism in Canada, Australia and South Africa, even in Ireland at last, and were thereby better equipped to meet its demands in Asia and Africa. Yet a doubt persists. There is something a little worrying perhaps in the readiness with which the British despatched their subjects into independence and reconciled themselves (if indeed they have) to the end of Empire. The actual conversion of Empire into Commonwealth was very creditable, very poised, generous and well-mannered; yet it showed too how willing the British were to free themselves of their ties with others. Other empires at least can claim to have opened their parliament and government to those of their overseas subjects whom they were prepared to welcome as nationals by adoption. The British would not do so—until the limited and abortive proposals for integration with Malta; and then only with great heart searchings. One can understand their uneasiness in terms of the delicate balance and continuity of political life in Britain—once the Irish had withdrawn. (The French, after all, have always had fewer institutions at a political level to preserve.) And if critical observations of this kind were simply a judgement on British colonial rule they would not matter: a Commonwealth of Nations is no bad end to Empire. But one may wonder—and in so short an essay one can do no more than wonder—whether this deep-rooted belief in the right of self-determination, and the protective exclusion even of those most like themselves, will stand the British in such good stead in the future, when the inviolability of their institutions and political life may not be so easy to preserve in the context of Europe as in the high and palmy state of empire.

MAP OF THE MALTESE ISLANDS

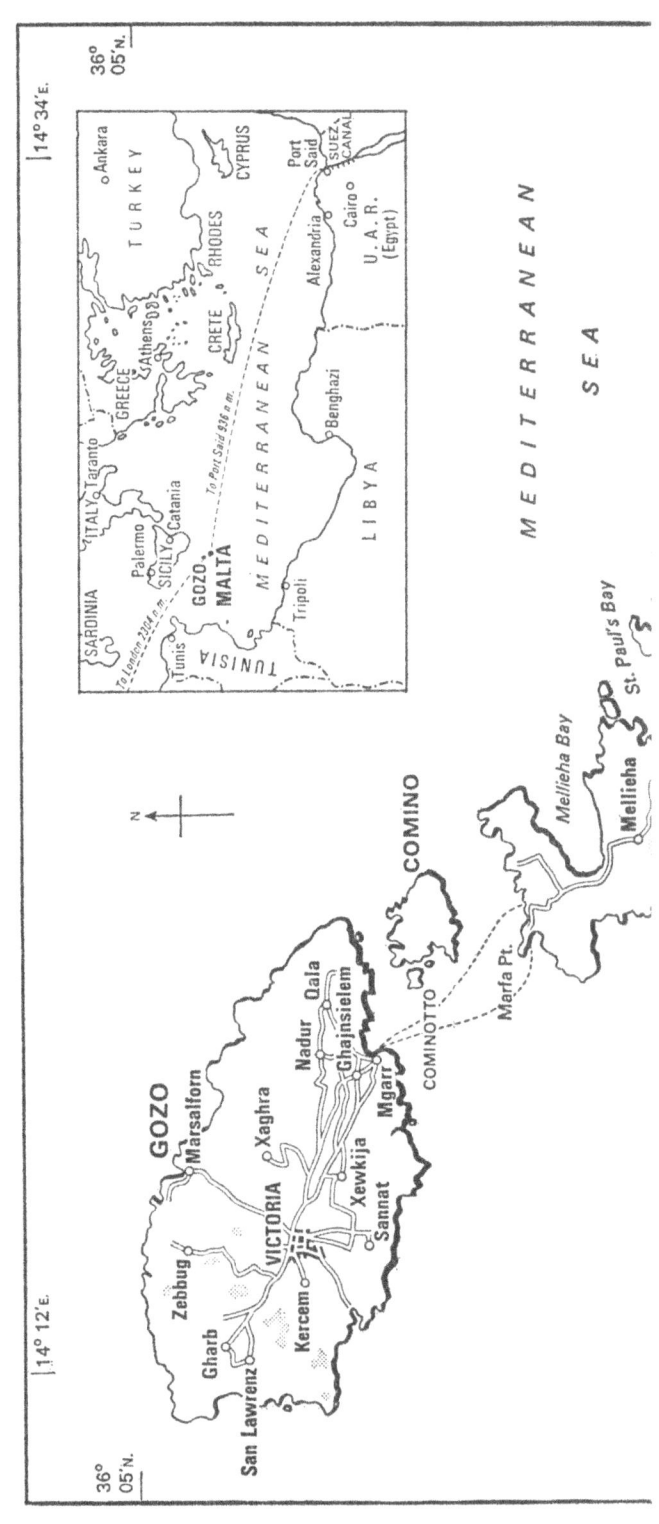

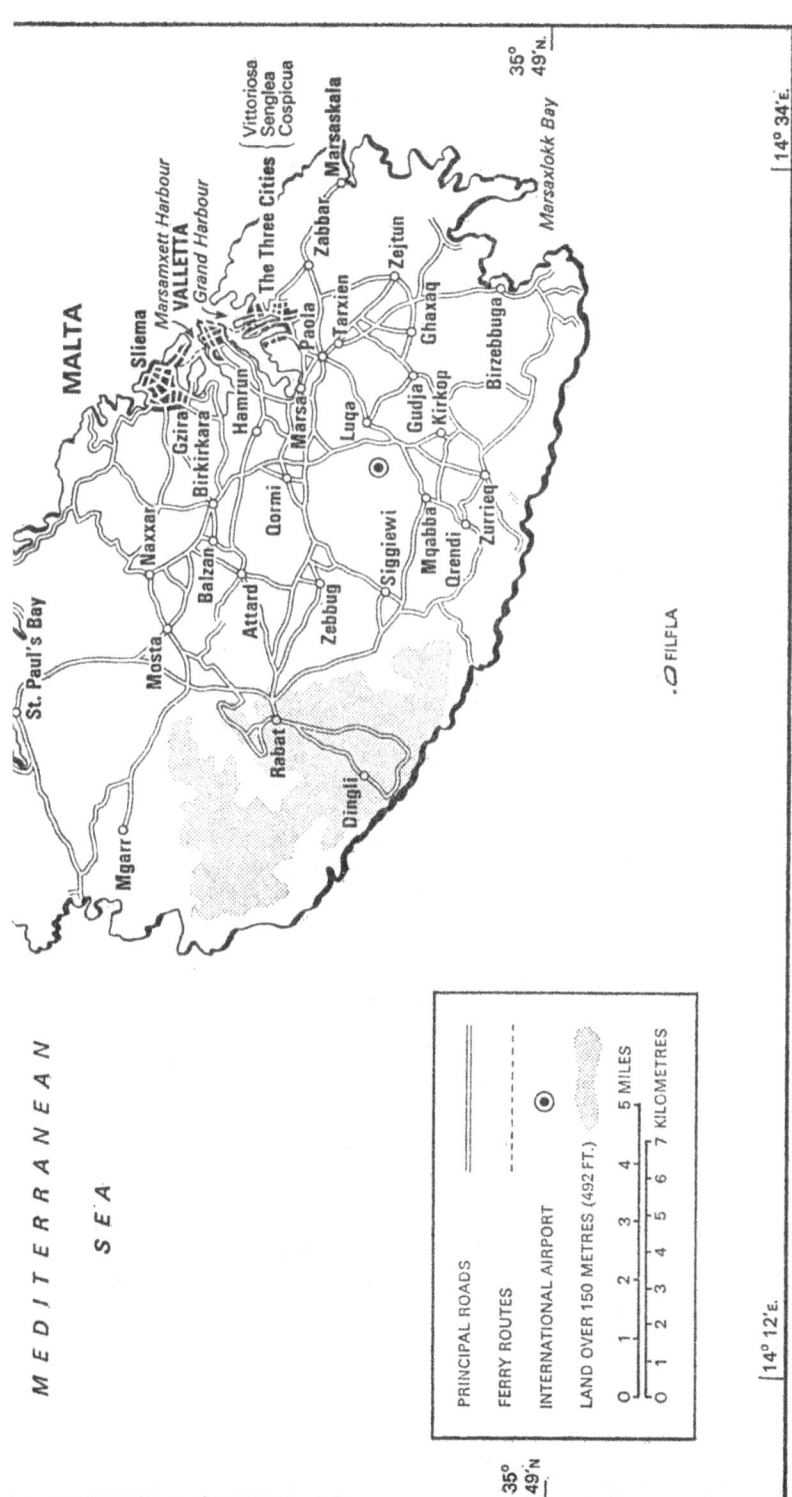

Notes

PART I

[1] Uninhabited except by a unique, dark-green lizard with red spots (*lacerta muralis*).

[2] *Census Reports, 1968*.

[3] The Carthaginian general Hamilcar surrendered to the Roman Consul, Titus Sempronius, in Malta in 216 BC, in the circumstances related by Livy (Bk. XXI. 5); Diodorus Siculus, as late as the first century AD, writes of Malta as "a colony of Phoenicians". Hence St. Luke's use of the term *barbaroi* for the islanders (Acts XXVII) in the sense that they were neither Roman nor Hellenic. The Maltese language is still something of a mystery. Its defenders claim that it is the ancient language of Carthage, Tyre and Sidon; less friendly critics argue that it is a debased form of Arabic. A more generous view might be that it is basically Punic in structure with the addition of Arabic, Sicilian, Italian and English words; see A. E. Caruana, *Sull' origine della lingua Maltese* (1896); Hancock, *Survey of Commonwealth Affairs* (1937), Vol. I, 422; Joseph Aquilina, *The Structure of Maltese* (1951); and *Papers in Maltese Linguistics* (The Royal University of Malta, Valletta, 1961).

[4] As in Ovid's day: "Fertilis est Melite sterili vicina Cosyrae/Insula, quam Libyci verberat unda freti". Cosyra is Pantelleria.

[5] Malta was never ruled directly by the Byzantine empire, but the islands were much influenced by the neighbouring Greek colony in Sicily.

[6] As under the Romans to whom the Maltese were *dedititii* and, according to Cicero who ruled in Malta as quaestor in 75 BC, *socii*. The first British Governor (1813-24) was Sir Thomas Maitland.

Notes: Part I

[7] The knights were grouped into eight *langues*: Auvergne, Provence, France, Aragon, Castile, Italy, Germany and (for a time) England, each with its *auberge* or headquarters.

[8] During the early years of the *Risorgimento* a number of its leading figures took shelter in Malta, among them Crispi, Pilo and Fabrizzi. By the 1850's, Malta was the armoury for Sicily, weapons being shipped there by Mazzini in London. See G. M. Trevelyan, *Garibaldi and the Thousand* (Harmondsworth, 1965), p. 142.

[9] Founded as a College of the Society of Jesus by Bishop Fra Tommaso Gargallo in 1592. The old buildings in St. Paul's Street, Valletta, date from 1585, the College being raised to the official status of a University by Grand Master Emmanuel Pinto in 1769 and named the Royal University of Malta in 1937. The foundation stone of the new buildings at Tal Qrogg, Msida, was laid in 1964.

[10] A word of explanation is needed here. The first legislative council was established in 1835, then reconstituted in 1849 with 8 elected and 10 official plus nominated members. It was enlarged in 1887 to provide for an "unofficial majority"— 8 officials (including the Governor), 14 elected from single member constituencies and 4 special members for the nobility, clergy, chamber of commerce, and the university. Provision was also made for 3 or more unofficial members on the executive of ten. A familiar constitution, but with special Maltese features: (1) a limit of two was imposed on the number of priests who might be elected among the 10 open seats; (2) these were always Maltese *officials* as well as unofficials; (3) the *scrutin de liste* was abolished in 1888 in favour of single member constituencies and a preferential, transferable vote method of election; (4) the early mode of opposition adopted by Fortunato Mizzi, Azzopardi, Panzavecchio and others was peculiar: when they objected *in toto* to government policy they resigned and secured the election in their stead of near-illiterates and rascals to bring the council into confusion. The 1887 constitution lasted until 1903, when Malta reverted to the position in 1849—until 1921, when it moved forward again.

[11] The 1921 constitution was as follows: [A] A Maltese Government consisting of a Senate of 17—8 special members,

7 members elected on a limited franchise, and 2 members chosen by the trade unions; their term of office was 6 years; a Legislative Assembly of 32 elected on a generous franchise; an Executive Council of 7 Ministries. [B] The Maltese Imperial Government under the Governor assisted by a nominated council of the Lt. Governor, the legal adviser, and the 3 heads of the armed forces. [C] A Privy Council (summoned at the discretion of the Governor) consisting of the Executive Council and the nominated Council.

The first prime ministers were compromise candidates: Joseph Howard (1921-3) and Dr. Buhagiar (1923-4).

[12] Sir Ugo Mifsud was Prime Minister 1924-27, 1932-3. The Nationalist Party was formed by Mizzi in January 1926 by the merger of Panzavecchio's *Unione Politica* with the *Partito Nazionalista Democratico* led by Mizzi. Sir Ugo Mifsud could also express himself fiercely about British rule at times, as in his election speech on 24 October 1932: " La storia dei Dominii dimonstra che, quando L'Inghilterra dà della libertà a gente che non è del proprio sangue, le dà dietro lotta. Il capo Guidice de Quebec mi disse una volta: L'Inghilterra vi dà le libertà quando non può piu stringere'. E posso dire che le libertà ce l'hanno date, perchè non potevano piu stringere."

[13] Quoted in Hancock, Vol. I, p. 427 f.2.

[14] Strickland's father was Captain Strickland, R.N., his mother a member of the Maltese nobility, the title—Count della Catena—having been bestowed by Grand Master Pinto in 1745.

[15] Becoming Lord Strickland and a member of the House of Lords in 1928.

[16] Luke, *Cities and Men*, p. 62.

[17] Cmd. 3993, 1931.

[18] The Church and the Nationalists were not always in league together. Fortunato Mizzi had once been dubbed *homo inimicus* by the Archbishop-Bishop of Malta: but the two sides came close together in opposition to Strickland and, helped by the Lateran Treaty between Mussolini and the Vatican in 1929, were close allies throughout the 1930s.

Notes : Part I

Strickland was much harassed by rumours (spread by his opponents) vilifying the leaders of the Constitutional and Labour parties, including the quite unfounded but (in Maltese eyes) horrendous charge that Strickland was a Freemason. Strickland's account of the campaign may be found in his speech in the House of Lords, 25 June, 1930.

[19] See Luke, *Cities and Men,* p. 63, Hancock, p. 412 ff, and the documents in *Correspondence with the Holy See relative to Maltese Affairs, Jan. 1929-May 1930.* Blue Book, Cmnd. 3588.

[20] Founded in April 1921; it was in alliance under Dr. Paul Boffa with Strickland, 1927-32.

[21] Quoted in Cmd. 3588 p. 66-8.

[22] Cmd. 3993, 1931. Members were Lord Askwith, Sir Walter Egerton and the Count de Salis.

[23] Seats and Votes

	1927		1932	
	1st Preference Votes	Seats	1st Preference Votes	Seats
Nationalist Party	15,079	14	28,906	21
Constitutionalists	14,130	15	14,513	10
Labour Party	4,773	3	4,221	1

[24] The reasons given by the Secretary of State, Sir Philip Cunliffe-Lister, were as follows: "The House will remember that when responsible government was restored in 1932 it was made subject to certain stipulations regarding the languages to be taught in the elementary schools. It was laid down that in these schools the children should be instructed in Maltese and English only, adequate provision being made for the teaching of Italian in the secondary schools. . . . Unfortunately by a series of actions of which the cumulative effect is unmistakable, the Maltese Ministers have made it clear that the main object of their policy has been to frustrate the effective operation of the conditions." They had also overspent their financial vote, particularly on the teaching of Italian. And the Governor had "assumed the administration of the Island in virtue of a provision inherent in the Constitution by which, in the event of a local emergency, he is

Malta and the End of Empire

entitled to invoke his reserved powers." H.C. Deb. 7 Nov., 1933.

[25] Except indirectly and at a distance, for Mizzi continued to attack the government in his paper *Malta,* and Strickland condemned the suspension of the Constitution on every possible occasion in the House of Lords.

[26] Dom Mintoff, *Priests and Politics in Malta,* 1961, p. 3. "The Second World War saw the Maltese clergy work hand in glove with the British Government. Not only were the old pro-Italian days forgiven and forgotten; from pulpit and square the priests preached to the faithful and extolled the righteousness of Britain's cause." The fact is however that the Labour Party actively supported the colonial administration during the 1930s because of its welfare legislation.

[27] The greater part of the service was in Maltese hands—under Colonial direction.

[28] Hancock, p. 427.

[29] Hancock, p. 428.

[30] Luke, p. 71.

[31] *Ibid*. p. 73.

[32] Hancock, p. 429. Again there were precedents: Strickland had introduced a series of school books in the Maltese language (printed from Roman characters, with translations in English underlined in different type), produced at the Government Printing Office and sold at cost price, as early as the 1900s.

[33] Churchill, *The Second World War* (1962), Vol. III, p. 687. "You may be sure that we regard Malta as one of the master keys of the British Empire." (Prime Minister to Governor of Malta, 6 June, 1941.)

[34] An interim constitution had already been introduced in 1939 establishing a Council of Government of 10 elected, 2 nominated and 8 official members. The ten elected were Dr. Boffa, Lord Strickland, Major Roger Strickland, A. V. Bartolo, Dr. Borg, Anthony Montano, Dr. Sacco, Sir Ugo Mifsud, Dr. Mizzi and a new Nationalist Party Leader—Dr. Borg Olivier. There were further elections in 1945, boycotted by the Nationalists.

Notes : Part I

[35] The Governor had his own officers—the Lieutenant Governor, Legal Secretary, Director of Civil Aviation, and the Secretary to the "Maltese Imperial Government". He was also obliged to consult a Nominated Council of advisers in respect of the reserved subjects.

[36] Cmd. 9657. Eden's statement announcing the convening of a conference was made on 6 July, 1955.

[37] A Minority Report, signed by Mr. John MacKay and Mr. Kenneth Pickthorn, argued the need for caution, particularly in granting parliamentary representation on the basis of an unequal responsibility. See Part II above. Lord Perth (a Catholic) added a special rider to paragraph 79 of the main Report stressing the need for "appropriate and satisfactory assurances" about the rights of the Church in Malta over "education and family life".

PART II

[1] T. Balogh and D. Seers, *The Economic Problems of Malta* (Valetta, 1955). See, too, Sir G. Schuster, *Interim Report on the Financial and Economic Structure of the Maltese Islands* (1950) (Col. No. 260).

[2] 15 April, 1943 and again in July 1944. By the following year, the *Times* had shelved the idea as being not feasible for the immediate future, not least because of its dismissal by Oliver Stanley. Mr. Miller of the General Workers Union was also to claim later that he had advocated integration with Britain in the same year—1943.

[3] The Memorandum was printed later in the *Times of Malta*, 3 December, 1953. One of the grievances it expressed was over the allocation of seats to the Maltese Government at the coronation of Queen Elizabeth: Dr. Boffa had been placed among the Dominion (and Rhodesian) Prime Ministers at the wedding of Princess Elizabeth and Prince Philip: now in 1953 at the Coronation Dr. Olivier (and Malta) were relegated to the ranks of the colonial and dependent territories. The "Maltese Prime Minister insisted, though without justification by the protocol, that he must drive in the procession with the Prime Ministers of the self-governing Dominions. I had at first refused this privilege but . . . the Prime Minister conceded it, perhaps rightly." Then it was found there were no trained horses to pull the carriage. "The horse crisis lasted for a day or two. The Equerry said that he could only throw in his reserve of two upon the direct order of the Queen. I said, 'The horses to draw this carriage have become a matter of imperial policy. Would you ask the Queen?' Her Majesty took the very real risk, and released them." *Memoirs of Lord Chandos* (London, 1962), p. 427. Of such stuff are empires and Commonwealths made!

[4] H.C. Deb. 9 December, 1953.

Notes: Part II

[5] Borg Olivier's coalition government was defeated in the Maltese Assembly in October, resigned, but returned to power in December, 1953. See above p. 23.

[6] It was not until the passing of the *loi cadre* on 19 January, 1956 that any substantial autonomy was given to the French Overseas Territories in tropical Africa and Madagascar. Even then it was much less than that possessed by Malta in 1947 —or 1921. Hawaii—and Alaska—were represented in the House of Representatives in Washington each by a single elected delegate who could speak but not vote; there was a local legislature in each territory under an appointed Governor: both territories however were on their way to full federal statehood. Puerto Rico was similarly placed, though not an "incorporated territory"; representation at Washington was through an elected Resident Commissioner. Puerto Ricans were American citizens but "joined" to the United States in the form of a "compact" under the Puerto Rican Federal Relations Act of July 1950 which designated Puerto Rico a "Commonwealth". See Kenneth Robinson, *Political Studies*, Vol. IV, No. 3, October 1956.

[7] It was suggested that there should be two joint consultative committees: one in Valletta with equal representation on the one hand of the Malta Government and, on the other, of the United Kingdom Service Departments and the Home Office (to which responsibility for Maltese affairs would be transferred); the other in London, with United Kingdom and Maltese ministers, the former in the majority.

[8] That is, from the office of the Prime Minister.

[9] 1955 Election—149,378 registered voters. 1956 Referendum —152,823 registered voters.

[10] *Times of Malta,* 16 February, 1956.

[11] Similar arguments had been used by other Labour leaders: e.g. by Dr. Anton Buttigieg in the Maltese language newspaper *Is-Sebh* on 8 January, 1955.

[12] The leaders were not very different, however, from the Nationalist and Constitutionalist parties. A majority of them were from the "professional" or "administrative" class. See the table in Jeremy Boissevain's extremely interesting study of Maltese local politics, *Saints and Fireworks* (1965):

Occupation of Candidates Elected to the Legislative Assembly 1962

	Nat.	Labour	Other	Total	Percentage
Professional	24	9	5	38	76
Administrative	1	4	2	7	14
Skilled labour	0	3	2	5	10
	25	16	9	50	100

[13] Boissevain has a good account of the Labour Party in its local setting in *Saints and Fireworks,* Chs. VII and VIII. See, too, his article "Malta Village Politics and their relation to National Politics", *Journal of Commonwealth Political Studies,* Nov. 1962.

[14] Formed on 23 October, 1943 at a mass meeting in Valletta, out of the former Dockyard and Imperial Workers' Union. The G.W.U. newspapers—*The Torch* (a Sunday paper), *L-Orizzont* (daily), and the *Malta News* (daily)—have the largest circulation of any newspapers in Malta. The G.W.U. has no overt political affiliations—there is no political levy; but it "stands behind" the Labour Party on most issues. See R. Matrenza's paper in *Labour Unions and Political Organisations,* Instit. of Commonwealth Studies, London University, Jan.-May, 1967. In 1956 trade union membership was estimated at 24,861 of which the G.W.U. claimed 18,091 members.

[15] *Encounter,* a new and short-lived monthly magazine which appeared in February 1956, published by the "Young Nationalist Movement", Dr. Ganado had been interned in East Africa with Mizzi during the war. Between 1950 and 1964 he moved towards collaboration with the Malta Government.

[16] Dr. Felice, Broadcast, 2 February, 1956.

[17] 1947—19,041 votes
1950—31,431 votes
1951—39,946 votes
1953—45,180 votes
1955—48,514 votes

[18] I have used the past tense; but of course what was true

Notes: Part II

of Dr. Borg Olivier in 1955-6 is true today in 1970. He was born in 1911, educated at the Lyceum, Malta and the Royal University of Malta where he read law: elected to the Council of Government in 1939, he became deputy leader of the Nationalist Party and deputy leader of the Opposition in 1947, Prime Minister (after the death of Mizzi in December 1950) until 1955, Prime Minister again in February 1962 to the present time.

[19] A. Montanaro, Secretary PCP, Broadcast.

[20] Evidence submitted by Miss Strickland and Dr. Busuttil to the Round Table Conference. There was an amusing exchange between Mr. Attlee and Miss Strickland:

Mr. Attlee: Miss Strickland. I think you expressed some apprehension that if we had Maltese members at Westminster, Malta might not be brought to the fore in the House of Commons. I had the honour of sitting in the House of Commons with your revered father for a number of years and my recollection is that he showed great ingenuity in introducing the political controversies of Malta into every possible subject brought before the House.

Miss Strickland: So much so that the Conservative Party Whips tried to unseat him at Lancaster!

[21] *Voice of Malta,* 6 February.

[22] H.C. Deb., 1 Feb., 1956.

[23] Founded by the St. Paul's Apostolic Circle, Rabat.

[24] Whose head was Herbert Ganado.

[25] *Magister Ultinam Sequatus Evangelium Universus Mundus* —the Society of Christian Doctrine: "the strictest and one of the oldest of the lay apostolate groups . . . its members are now among the staunchest opponents of the Labour Party". Boissevain, p. 20-1.

[26] Report in the *Times of Malta,* 9 February, 1956.

[27] *Times of Malta,* 9 February, 1956.

[28] Omitting 2,559 invalid votes. Of those who voted, 14,461 voted by "proxy":—being illiterate, or otherwise unable to record their vote, they used "trusted persons" to vote for them, an innovation which was not repeated in subsequent contests.

[29] There was a wild flurry of threats and counter-threats in the immediate post-referendum period: it was known, for example, that some members of the Opposition had flown to Dublin, others to the Vatican, and Mintoff threatened to arm his supporters and withdraw police protection from the Opposition if they flirted "with the IRA or other foreign agents". (Victory Rally speech at the Stadium, 6 April, 1956.)

[30] The British reaction to the referendum is discussed in Part III.

[31] There is a number of long term projects in hand—water catchments, afforestation, a continuing campaign against undulant fever, a Gozo milk pasteurisation plant, etc.

[32] *Legislative Assembly Debates,* 4 April, 1956.

[33] *Malta Constitutional Conference. Documents relating to the Discussions held between the U.K. Delegation and the Malta Labour Party Delegation, in London, during November and December 1958.* See, too, Mintoff's pamphlet, *Malta Betrayed: Truncheons and Tyrants,* containing correspondence between the Malta Government and Britain, 8-23 April, 1958.

[34] See Appendix E, *Report of the Malta Constitutional Commission, 1960.* "Financial Aid given to Malta compared with some other territories 1957-8, 1959-60."

For these calculations population figures as shown in the 1960 Colonial Office List have been used. The total aid of the period has been taken from the Colonial Development and Welfare Fund, the Colonial Services Vote and Exchequer Loans. In the case of Malta only, aid amounting to approximately £10 per capita from War Damage Fund sources has been included.

	Per Capita	Population
St. Helena	89.23	4,802
Malta	50.46	323,667
Virgin Islands	44.02	7,600
British Honduras	34.97	88,281
Seychelles	16.41	43,149
Gibraltar	13.77	25,637
Kenya	1.76	6,450,000
Uganda	0.63	5,868,200
Mauritius	0.40	632,721

Notes: Part II

Malta had the highest per capita rate of Colonial Development and Welfare assistance promised in the period 1959-64 of all territories, followed by St. Helena, Gibraltar, Virgin Islands, Seychelles and British Honduras.

[35] H.C. Deb., 2 Feb., 1959.

[36] Circular issued from the Archbishop's Curia, 26 May, 1961.

[37] See Mintoff's angry comments in his pamphlet: "Mock Transfer of the Malta Dockyard to Baileys' (Malta, Union Press, n.d.), and *Report by Mr. J. B. Muirie on Bailey (Malta) Ltd., 15 August, 1962* (HMSO 1963).

[38] British troops were withdrawn from Aden in 1967; the decision to withdraw by 1971 from the Gulf and from southeast Asia was announced in January 1968.

PART III

[1] R. G. Hawtry, *Economic Aspects of Sovereignty* (London, 1952), p. 151, quoted in Kenneth Robinson, "The End of Empire", *International Affairs,* Vol. XXX, No. 2, April 1954.

[2] *The Modern Commonwealth,* HMSO, January 1962.

[3] Not books but volumes would be needed to sift the evidence for statements of this kind, but the rapid disappearance of the European empires is a plain enough fact. Somewhere during the 1950s Britain, Belgium and France gave up the Imperial ghost, and ceased to whimper on the grave thereof.

[4] 2 March, 1961.

[5] "Imperial Policy." *Conservative and Unionist Central Office,* June, 1949.

[6] H.C. Deb., 16 December, 1964. Vol. 704, Col. 423. Similar phrases appear in the *Statement on the Defence Estimates 1965,* Cmd., 5292, para. 7.

[7] "Wind of Change", *Conservative Political Centre Pamphlet No. 211,* April, 1960.

[8] I have foreshortened a complicated argument here, discussed by Kenneth Robinson—*il miglior fabbro*—in "Alternatives to Independence", *Political Studies,* Vol. IV, No. 3, October, 1956.

[9] As high as 30 per cent according to the *Report of the Constitutional Commission* by Sir Hilary Blood and others. Cmd. 1261, 1961, para. 35. These quotations are from Ch. IV of the report.

[10] For comparison, the comments in the *Encyclopaedia Britannica* of 1911 are interesting: "In appearance, the Maltese are a handsome, well-formed race, about the middle height, and well set up; they have escaped the negroid contamination noticeable in Sicily, and their features are less dark than the Southern Italians. . . . They are a thrifty and industrious people, prolific and devoted to their off-

Notes: Part III

spring, good-humoured, quick-tempered and impressionable ... enthusiastic observers of festivals, fasts and ceremonials."

[11] 28 September, 1886. *The Times* responded kindly in its editorial, comparing the Maltese with the Channel Islanders.

[12] e.g. *The 1960 Report of the Malta Constitutional Commission* (Cmd. 1261), para. 31. After further riots in 1958: "despite constant criticism directed at the Commission and its members in somewhat offensive terms by *Il Helsien* and *The Voice of Malta* ... during the whole period of our stay in Malta never once did we find this reflected in the attitude adopted towards us by the people themselves. On the contrary, we met nothing but the utmost friendliness from people in all walks of life with whom we came in contact."

[13] H.C. Deb., 26 March, 1956.

[14] The results of the 1966 general election are of some interest in showing the balance of party strength in and out of parliament:

	Votes	Seats
National Party	68,656	28
Labour Party	61,774	22
Others	12,918	0

The islands display their Englishness in other ways too. As the results of long contact with the Royal Navy and (in recent years) a growing tourist traffic, there is a strong flavour of English social life throughout the islands together with less public pleasures in the Snake Pit, and the Late Joe Blount's bar, the Britannia, and other friendly little bars along the water front.

[15] H.C. Deb., 26 March, 1956, Cols. 1778-1931, from which subsequent quotations are taken.

[16] The results of the 1948 referenda in Newfoundland were:

1st Referendum

For Responsible Government	69,230	(as before 1933)
For Confederation	63,110	(with Canada)
For Commission Government	21,944	(as after 1933)

2nd Referendum

For Responsible Government	71,334
For Confederation	78,323

See St. John Chadwick, *Newfoundland* (Oxford University Press, 1967).

[17] Kenneth Pickthorn (Carlton).

[18] The Archbishop, said Teeling, was not only "miserably unhappy and worried". He was also a power in the land. "He could have excommunicated people, and gone much further in many ways. . . . I warn the House that it must realise that these are facts. It is most unlikely that the Vatican will ever let the Archbishop down. I know a great deal about the way in which the Vatican works. It is immensely loyal to its Archbishops all over the world, and it has a deep affection and respect for this one."

[19] See p. 91.

[20] As in 1964 when the Labour Party had a majority of only 3 over its Conservative and Liberal opponents.

[21] Alas, poor Malta! A further test in 1956 would have meant seven contests in nine years: 6 elections and a referendum since 1947.

[22] *Full Circle*, pp. 388-9. Eden too was uneasy about the outcome of the referendum. It was "probably as good from Mr. Mintoff's point of view, as he expected, but nearly half the electorate had not voted. A question which could never be resolved was how many of the large number who abstained must be regarded as having been deterred by the strong advice given by the Church." *Ibid.* p. 388.

[23] 26 March, 1956.

[24] See, for example, comment in *The Methodist Recorder*—it would be "a scandal of the first magnitude" if integration went through without a change in the civil powers of the Catholic Church in Malta.

[25] Major General Sir Robert Laycock, 1954-59; Admiral Sir Guy Grantham, 1959-63; Sir Maurice Dorman, Governor 1963-64, Governor-General 1964 to the present time.

[26] Lennox Boyd, 1954-56; Iain Macleod, 1956-61; Duncan Sandys, 1962-64.

[27] Dobie, *Malta's Road to Independence* (1967), Chapters VIII to XI.

[28] Cmd. 1261. Sir Hilary Blood was appointed chairman of a commission of 4 appointed on 22 August, 1960; he submitted his recommendations in December 1960.

[29] *Voice of Truth*, published by Catholic Action.

Notes: Part III

[30] *Priests and Politics in Malta 1961.* The extent of the hostility between the Archbishop and Dom Mintoff can be seen from the letters exchanged between the Curia and the Labour Party executive in 1961, printed as a series of appendices in Mintoff's *Priests and Politics in Malta*, e.g. "The position reached to date is: (1) many priests refuse absolution to Labour supporters; (2) members of the National Executive are interdicted; (3) it is a mortal sin to read, sell, distribute Labour Party papers; (4) priests urge "good" Catholics to break up Labour Party public meetings whilst church bells are rung incessantly to drown the voices of Labour speakers; (5) 'reparation' squads of priests turn up with icons and statues in the same locality where Labour had held public meetings; the priests blacken with impunity the reputation of their opponents; (6) even corpses do not escape the witch-hunt: the family of the dead leader of the Malta Labour Party were not allowed to bury him in their own private grave. His grave lies in a small adjunct to the national cemetery which the 'faithful' have nicknamed the refuse-heap."

[31] Borrowed from the "recently created internally self-governing State of Singapore". Cmd. 1261 Ss 23.90.

[32] Clause 48(10) and (11) of Chapter IV of the draft "Constitution of Malta" published, for the purpose of the referendum, in *Malta Government Gazette*, April 1964, Valletta.

[33] It may be helpful here to reproduce the 1956 integration vote:

(1) Electorate	152,823		
(2) Voters	90,343	59%	
(3) For Integration	67,607	74% of (2), 44% of (1)	
(4) Against Integration	20,177	22% of (2)	85,216
(5) Spoiled Votes	2,559	4% of (2)	= 56% of (1)
(6) Non-Voters	62,480	—	

[34] H.C. Deb., 23 July, 1964. Subsequent quotations are from the same source.

[35] Letter in *The Guardian*, 23 July, from Count Michael de la Bedoyere, former editor of the *Catholic Herald*, who drew comparisons between the Church in Malta and the reforms proposed by Pope John.

Malta and the End of Empire

[36] "Grudging acceptance" is surely the right description of Bottomley's remarkable message of good will. "We wish the people of Malta well. We say that the Government of Malta have a heavy responsibility . . . serving as a government for a short time I hope, so that after another election, like the one we are shortly to have in this country, a Government to the liking of the people of Malta will be in power. I would prefer that to have been done before independence but I hope that soon after independence there will be a General Election in Malta. On behalf of my party, I wish God-speed to Malta."

[37] Lord Perth tried to block the passage of the Bill by moving an amendment requiring a further election or referendum before independence. That too was rejected by Conservative and Labour peers alike.

[38] Duncan Sandy's phrase: "We could, of course, pitchfork all our colonial territories into independence overnight, as some members of the United Nations are pressing us to do. But we consider we have a responsibility to the inhabitants, which we must fully discharge. We have a duty, not only to lead them to independence, but also to prepare them for the responsibilities which this involves," *The Modern Commonwealth* (HMSO, 1961), p. 4.

[39] Guadeloupe—585 square miles; 229,120 population.
Martinique—385 square miles; 239,130 population.
Réunion—967 square miles; 274,370 population.
Malta—122 square miles; 314,175 population.

[40] J. A. Roebuck, quoted approvingly by Gladstone in 1885.

[41] Lord Hailey's phrase. "The instinct of the British [unlike the French or Roman Empire] is to attach to the grant of political rights the importance which others have given to the acquisition of social and cultural equality. . . . We should fail to discharge the duty of a trustee did we not give to our dependent peoples the fullest opportunities for developing their own sense of national consciousness and for acquiring the control of their own affairs." Romanes Lectures, 1941.

[42] A point noted by R. G. Collingwood in his comparison between the Roman and British Empires. See his very interesting remarks in *Roman Britain* (Oxford, 1934), Chapter I.

Select Bibliography

I *Books and Pamphlets*

Beeley, B. W.	*A Bibliography of the Maltese Islands*. Durham, 1960.
Boissevain, Jeremy.	*Saints and Fireworks: Religion and Politics in Rural Malta*. London, 1965.
Bowen-Jones, Howard.	*Malta: Background for Development*. Durham, 1961.
Bradfield, E.	*The Great Siege of Malta*. London, 1961.
Dobie, Edith.	*Malta's Road to Independence*. Oklahoma, 1967.
Eden, Sir Anthony.	*Full Circle*. London, 1960.
Evans, John.	*Malta*. London, 1959.
Gulia, Wallace.	*Local Government in Malta*. Malta, 1967.
Hancock, W. K.	*Survey of British Commonwealth Affairs*. London, 1937.
Kininmonth, Christopher.	*The Brass Dolphins*. London, 1957.
Laferla, A. V.	*British Malta*, Vol. 1, 1800-1872; Vol. 2, 1872-1921. Malta, 1947.
Laferla, A. V.	*The Story of Man in Malta*. Malta, 1958.
Luke, Sir Harry.	*Cities and Men, An Autobiography*. London, 1956.
Luke, Sir Harry.	*Malta: an Account and an Appreciation*. London, 1960.
Mintoff, Dom.	*Malta's Struggle for Survival*. Malta, 1949.
Mintoff, Dom.	*Malta Betrayed: Truncheons and Tyrants*. Malta, n.d.

Malta and the End of Empire

Mintoff, Dom.	*Mock Transfer of the Malta Dockyard to Bailey.* Malta, n.d.
Mintoff, Dom.	*Priests and Politics in Malta.* Malta, 1961.
Price, Charles A.	*Malta and the Maltese: A Study in Nineteenth Century Migration.* Melbourne, 1954.
Smith, Harrison.	*Britain in Malta,* Vols. I & II. Malta, 1953.
Strickland, Lord.	*Malta and the Phoenicians.* Malta, 1950.
Strickland, Mabel.	*Maltese Constitutional and Economic Issues, 1955-59.* Malta, 1959.

II *Recent Documents*

Malta: Recent Requests for Financial and Economic Assistance, Col. No. 253, HMSO 1949.

Interim Report on the Financial and Economic Structure of the Maltese Islands, by Sir George Schuster. Col. No. 260, HMSO 1950.

Economic Problems of Malta, by T. Balogh and D. Seers, Malta, 1955.

Malta Round Table Conference 1955 Report, Cmd. 9657, HMSO 1955.

Report of the Economic Commission, Col. No. 332, HMSO 1957.

Report of the Malta Constitutional Commission 1960, Cmd. 1261, HMSO 1961.

Malta Constitutional Conference, Documents relating to the Discussions held between the U.K. Delegation and the Malta Labour Party Delegation during November and December 1958. Malta 1959.

Malta (Constitutional) Order in Council 1961. HMSO 1963.

Malta (Constitutional) Order in Council 1964. HMSO 1964.

Report by Mr. J. B. Muirie on Bailey (Malta) Ltd., 1962. HMSO 1963.

Index

Aid, to Malta: 22, 34, 56–8, 100, table of comparisons, 122–3
Askwith Commission (1930): 12
Attlee, C. R.: 24, quoted 121
Bailey, Messrs. C. H.: *see* Dockyard
Balogh, T.: 27, quoted 89, 130
Bartolo, Dr. Augusto: 10, 116
Bevan, Aneurin: 24, quoted 73–4, 75, 77, 81
Blood, Sir Hilary: and 1961 constitution, 94, 96, 124
Boffa, Sir Paul: 9, 115, Coronation "crisis" 118
Boissevain, Jeremy: quoted 119–120, 121, 129
Bottomley, Arthur: quoted on 1964 referendum 100, 102, and on independence 128
Church, condemns Strickland 11–12, opposes integration 48–51, takes part in 1962 election 94–5, and 1964 constitution 98, interdict on Labour Party Executive 127
Churchill, Sir Winston: quoted 116
Constitution of Malta: early history 8–15, 113, 116, (1947) 20–1, (1961) 94, (1964) 99–100
Creasy, Sir Gerald: quoted 30
Crossman, R. S.: 24, quoted 74, 78, 79–80, 84, 86
Cunliffe-Lister, Sir Philip: quoted 18–19, 115–6
Cyprus: compared with Malta 58, 72, 74, 81–3
Dobie, Edith: 93, 126, 129
Dockyard: employment 27–8, 56, 59–60, 123, 130
Driberg, Thomas: criticises A.Bp Gonzi 101

Eden, Sir Anthony: quoted on Round Table Report 88, and on (1956) referendum 126
Edinburgh, Duke of: quoted 102
Elections: early record 23, 115, (1962) 94–5, 120–1, (1966) 125
Eliot, T. S.: quoted frontispiece, 63
Elliot, Walter: 24, quoted 74–5, 83
Felice, Dr.: quoted 41
France: and integration 105–8, 119
Ganado, Dr. Herbert: quoted 41, 120–1
General Workers Union: supports integration 37, 40, and 1962 election 95, 118, membership 120
Gibraltar: 83–4, 104
Gonzi, Sir Michael: 11, career 46, quoted 47–8, 97, criticised by Mintoff 95, 127, and by Driberg 101 See *Church*
Griffiths, James: quoted 76–7, 80–1, 87, opposes independence 101
Hawtrey, R. G.: quoted 65
Hancock, Sir Keith: quoted 17, 19
Hailey, Lord: quoted 128
Jenkins, Roy: quoted 71, 80
Knights of St. John: 4–6, 113
Knox-Cunningham: quoted 79
Lennox-Boyd, Alan: quoted frontispiece, on assurances to A.Bp 48, criticises Mintoff 55–8, quoted 75, 82, hesitates over integration 87, 126
Luke, Sir Harry: quoted 10, 19

Mackay, John: 24, 86, Minority Report to Round Table Conference 117

Malta Labour Party: and integration 37, character 39, 119–120, loses 1962 election 95–6, relations with Workers Union 120, loses 1966 election 125, See Mintoff

Maltese: language 17–19, 21, 112; and people 20, 68-71, 125

Matrenza, Richard: xii, 120

Mifsud, Sir Ugo: 8, quoted 114, 116

Miller, R. G.: quoted 37, 118

Mintoff, Dom: 21, quarrels with Boffa 22, becomes prime minister 23, proposes integration 23–4, 31–32, satisfaction with 1956 referendum 34–6, quoted 37, 48, 51, begins to turn against integration 53 seq., loses 1962 election 95, opposes referendum on independence 97–8, quoted 116, 122, 127

Mizzi, Enrico: 7–9, prime minister 23, 26, 41, 116

Mizzi, Fortunato: 7–8, 113, 114

Nationalist Party: origins 21, 26, views on integration 29–30, 40–1, 44, moves towards independence 94, increase in membership 120

Olivier, Borg: memorandum on integration 29, as leader 44, letters to *The Times* 89, becomes prime minister 95–6, early career 116, 121

Pastoral Letter: (1930) 11, (1956) 47

Perham, Margery: 83, quoted 90-1

Perth, Lord: 24, Rider to Round Table Report 117, opposes independence 128

Pickthorn, Kenneth: 24, quoted 76, Minority Report to Round Table Conference 117

Progressive Constitutionalist Party: and integration 44–5, and elections 95–6, 97–8, 125. See *Strickland, Mabel*

Ragonesi, Dr. V.: quoted 66

Referenda: (1956) results 33–5, (1964) 96–8, in Newfoundland 125

Risorgimento: 7, 113

Robinson, Kenneth: xi, 119, 124

Round Table Conference: Report (1955) quoted 24, 27, 28, outline of proposals 32–3

Saints and Fireworks: 119–120, 121

Sandys, Duncan, quoted 65, agrees to referendum on independence 96, argues against referendum results 99, insists on independence 102, 104, 126

Scarlet Pimpernel: quoted on 1956 referendum 38–9

Sempronius: reply to Scarlet Pimpernel 42–44

Strickland, Lord: 9–13, 114–6

Strickland, Mabel: suggests integration 28, opposes integration 45–6, quoted 121

Teeling, William: quoted 78–9, 83, 126

War (1939–45): Award of George Cross 19–20, 27

Wilson, Harold: quoted 67

For Product Safety Concerns and Information please contact our EU
representative GPSR@taylorandfrancis.com
Taylor & Francis Verlag GmbH, Kaufingerstraße 24, 80331 München, Germany

www.ingramcontent.com/pod-product-compliance
Lightning Source LLC
Chambersburg PA
CBHW070837020526
44114CB00041B/1950